PROFILES
OF
DECEPTION

How The News Media
Are Deceiving
The American People

Reed Irvine
and
Cliff Kincaid

Book Distributors, Inc.

Published by Book Distributors, Inc., Smithtown, New York
Manufactured in the United States of America

ISBN 0-9625053-0-7

Contents

The AIM Story

For 20 years Accuracy in Media has been focusing the public's attention on one-sided, inaccurate, biased and dishonest news reporting.

Founded in 1969 by Reed Irvine, it's *Accuracy in Media* column now calls attention to news media mischief and misdeeds all year long in newspapers reaching over one million people. Five times a week its *Media Monitor* radio broadcasts are carried on over 250 radio stations across the country. And twice every month Reed Irvine's *AIM Report* newsletter is mailed to subscribers and leading opinion makers in the country.

Reed Irvine is, today, America's best known and most highly respected news critic. He has appeared repeatedly on many TV programs such as the *Phil Donahue Show*, Ted Koppel's *Nightline, Crossfire, Good Morning America*, etc. and he lectures all over America.

Victor Lasky, columnist and author, says of him, "Reed Irvine is a modern-day David fighting Goliath—the most powerful institution in America today—the media." Charles Seib, former Ombudsman at *The Washington Post*, which Reed Irvine finds reason to criticize repeatedly for biased and one-sided news coverage, writes, "It sticks in my craw, but I'll say it. Irvine and his AIM are good for the press."

Cliff Kincaid is a veteran media critic who is also a journalist, having graduated with a degree in journalism from the University of Toledo, Ohio. He hosts a talk show on WNTR-AM *Newstalk* 1050 radio, heard Monday-Friday from 10:00 a.m. to noon in the Washington, D.C. area. He reports on media issues for *Human Events,* the national conservative weekly, and the *New York City Tribune.* He is the Washington columnist for *Between the Lines,* a California-based newsletter that monitors the press and Hollywood. He has appeared on numerous radio and television programs but is perhaps best remembered for his work several years ago as a substitute for Patrick J. Buchanan on CNN's *Crossfire* program. He is still heard on Accuracy in Media's radio commentary program, *Media Monitor*.

On the following pages are over one hundred of the columns and *Media Monitor* radio broadcasts written by Reed Irvine and Cliff Kincaid over the past three years. They have been selected because of the special way they reveal exactly how the news media have deceived the American people. You will be amazed at how often you have been misled about many news stories you remember.

Preface

A majority of the American people no longer trust the news media. They believe most news reporting is biased, one-sided, unfair and that the goal of reporters and editors is all too often to persuade the public to think as they do, not to give the public the straight facts and let them reach their own conclusions. This has been very clearly shown by public opinion polls.

A few years ago, a Gallup poll found that only twenty percent of those surveyed said they believed all or most of what they saw on the television news programs, and only seventeen percent believed all or most of what they read in newspapers. This is a sad state of affairs for an institution that plays such an important role in our democratic society.

Yet these feelings of mistrust are far from new. The feeling that the media were not giving the American people a fair shake erupted in manifestations of hostility toward the media at the 1964 Republican National Convention, where Barry Goldwater was nominated. Then, in September 1969, Vice President Agnew delivered a stinging condemnation of network television news in a speech in Des Moines, Iowa. It evoked the biggest flood of mail to ABC, CBS and NBC that they had ever seen and the letters, telegrams and calls were overwhelmingly supportive of Agnew's criticisms.

Viewer antagonism to the news media erupted again in 1988 after Dan Rather's now famous interview of George Bush on the CBS *Evening News*. Rather and his staff had worked for over a month on a plan to trap Bush into making damaging statements about his knowledge of the Iran arms affair on the eve of the Iowa caucuses. The Vice President was lured into the carefully prepared ambush on the pretense that Rather wanted to do a campaign profile on him.

Bush wisely insisted on a live, unedited interview, a precaution that saved his neck. He fought back after viewing the special six-minute report that the CBS News staff had prepared as a lead-in to the interview. It was devoted entirely to inconsistencies or allegedly unanswered questions relating to the Vice President's statements about the Iran arms affair. Bush made it clear that he felt he had been deceived about the purpose of the interview. He tried without success to steer it into other topics. Rather interrupted him, twenty times by actual count. Rather's aggressive rudeness shocked and offended many viewers, and they made their feelings known in calls and letters to the stations and to CBS headquarters in New York.

What is behind this kind of biased, unfair, manipulative news reporting? Surveys have shown that two-thirds of the journalists who write and edit our daily newspapers, our major news magazines, and our television network news programs are liberal in their political and social views. One survey of journalists working for our most influential news organizations found that over eighty percent of them had voted for the Democratic party candidate in every presidential election from 1964 through 1976. The Newspaper Guild, the union that represents the journalists who work for the print media, regularly endorses the Democratic presidential candidates, while the voters have shown their preference for the Republican candidates by landslide margins.

For years, journalists used to ridicule the charges that they are overwhelmingly liberal in their views, but since the publication of these surveys they have had to acknowledge what they knew to be true all along. They are out of sync with the people they claim to speak for. But now they argue that their views do not influence the way they report the news. They say they are professionals who have learned how to be objective and fair in spite of their strongly held personal beliefs on controversial issues.

A great many Americans disagree. They sense that they are still getting biased reporting, that candidates and policies they favor are not getting fair treatment. Many feel that there is some kind of conspiracy on the part of the people who control the media to manipulate public opinion. They also feel, with good reason, that their complaints are unheeded. All too often, criticisms are ignored and even rudely brushed aside. Inaccurate stories go uncorrected even in our most prestigious papers. Television journalists rarely admit making an error and almost never make a correction. A person, company or group that is wronged by a newspaper at least has a chance of getting a letter of protest printed in the paper. Television, which 80% of the public relies on for "the news," has nothing comparable to letters to the editor. Broadcasters are supposed to serve the public convenience, interest and necessity, because they are licensed by the Federal Communications Commission. For years they were subject to the FCC's Fairness Doctrine. That required them to air all sides of controversial issues of public importance, if they discussed such issues on the air. However, the national networks looked upon that requirement as a minor nuisance, one that they could easily get around by putting what they called "fairness filler" into their documentaries. "Fairness filler" was a minimal courtesy to the other side of any controversial position the documentary was produced to promote.

Martin Carr, one of the best known producers of television documentaries, explained in a lecture at the University of Rochester in 1978, how he was able to give the impression of being fair without being fair. One technique, which he described in graphic detail, was to select as a spokesman for the opposing point of view an individual who would hurt his side more than he would help it because of his personal style or characteristics. Carr said very candidly that if his audience did not feel as he did about the subject of a documentary after having seen it, he had failed. The purpose of TV documentaries was to persuade, to convince, not to provide both sides and let the viewers make up their own minds. A producer could not be sure of winning the audience to his point of view, if he permitted each side a fair and equal hearing.

If it surprises you that a producer would use such a technique to manipulate public opinion, consider this: a major TV network's program on *Hunger In America* once showed a tiny baby starving to death, but the footage was actually of a 2-1/2 pound premature baby. The purpose of the program was to convince viewers that America is uncaring.

All television reporting and print reporting is not as deceptive as that. This book is not concerned about run-of-the-mill stories, or those that have no serious impact on either public policy or personal reputations. It is concerned about information that has an important influence on public attitudes, behavior and policies.

All too often such information is badly flawed or misleadingly incomplete. What probably is worse, much of the information that the public needs in order to make intelligent decisions is overlooked or deliberately suppressed by the media. This has resulted in costly, even tragic, consequences.

Deceptive reporting on the Vietnam War had a strong bearing on the fact that our side lost. Millions of Vietnamese, Cambodians and Laotians died or were driven into exile as a result. The veteran New York Times correspondent, editor and columnist James Reston wrote immediately after the fall of Saigon that "the reporters and cameramen brought the issue of the war to the people, before Congress and the courts, and forced the withdrawal of American power from Vietnam." When Reston wrote that in April 1975, he was confident that all of this was to the credit of the journalists, even though this was accomplished by what other journalists have decried as being distorted reporting.

Ian Ward, who covered the war for *The London Daily Telegraph,* said in 1972 that the reporting had reached unprecedented levels of distortion, both deliberate and unintentional. He said that, as a result, the Western press had emerged as the most effective weapon in the enemy's arsenal.

Ward was far from alone in that judgment. Novelist Robert Elegant, a former war correspondent for *The Los Angeles Times,* has said much the same thing. Their views have been backed up by the former Viet Cong Minister of Justice, Truong Nhu Tang, who now lives in exile in Paris. In an AIM film on Vietnam he said that although the Viet Cong forces were decimated in the 1968 Tet Offensive, they won on the diplomatic and psychological fronts and, above all, on what he called the "fourth front": the American mass media.

Jerry Rubin, one of the leaders of the anti-war movement, said that television was their best organizer. The lavish attention TV gave to the antics of the anti-Vietnam protesters helped swell their ranks. Dr. Ernest Lefever's monumental study, TV and National Defense, showed that in 1972 the CBS *Evening News* aired four times as many "critical mentions" of U.S. and South Vietnamese policies and performance in the war as "supportive mentions." CBS News was far more supportive of Communist North Vietnam than of our South Vietnamese ally.

This kind of reporting was a demonstration of how the views of the journalists influenced the way the news was being reported. There was an enormous disparity between the amount of coverage given to the massacre of a few hundred Viet Cong civilians by American combat troops at My Lai and the deliberate murder of some 5,000 South Vietnamese civilians by the Communists during their occupation of Hue in February 1968. The latter was barely reported. It was not even mentioned on the network news programs, and no pictures of the corpses exhumed from the mass graves were published in this country or shown on television until fifteen years later. That is why few Americans remember Hue, but My Lai is known even to young people not born at the time those events took place. The coverage was tailored to fit reporters' and editors' own strong prejudices and objectives.

Another similar case involved the suppression of information about the great man-made famine in the Ukraine in 1932 and 1933. Stalin confiscated grain from the peasants and prevented outsiders from bringing grain in, because he wanted to kill Ukrainian nationalism by killing people. It is estimated that as many as ten million died as a result. Reporters such as Walter Duranty, who covered the Soviet Union for *The New York Times*, knew this but they failed to tell the world. A State Department dispatch discovered recently revealed that Duranty had agreements with the Soviet leaders and the Times and that his reports always would reflect the official Soviet position, not his own. This highly influential reporter was, by agreement with his employer, nothing more than a spokesman for the Soviet regime. His reports and book did much to create pro-Soviet and pro-communist sentiment in this country during the 1930s.

Also, some media organizations have hired journalists, or used their material, despite strong evidence that they were under the control of foreign intelligence services. One was the late Wilfred Burchett, an Australian communist whose articles appeared from time to time in *The New York Times*, even after a KGB defector testified that he had recruited Burchett. The Times never identified him as a communist, much less as a KGB agent.

A few years ago, it was estimated that as many as ninety percent of the reporters working for the U.S. media in Nicaragua were Sandinista sympathizers. For that reason, the local people who opposed the regime distrusted American reporters and were afraid to talk openly with them. Today, we can see the consequences of their one-sided, manipulative reporting.

Exactly the opposite situation exists in South Africa where most of the reporters are hostile to the government and to black moderates who oppose America's imposition of sanctions. Two years ago, a group of moderate black clergymen came to this country to voice their opposition to sanctions legislation, but they could not get any publicity on network television or in major papers. When they were asked whether they were able to get their message across through American reporters in South Africa, one replied, "They wouldn't touch us with a broomstick." These ministers claimed to represent millions of black South Africans, far more than Archbishop Desmond Tutu, who regularly appears on American TV.

Day after day, this kind of distortion, deception and misinformation is part of the "News" the American people receive. The journalists are still slanting their stories and refusing to report or give adequate attention to news and views that clash with their idea of what is good for their readers and viewers to know. They remain wedded to ideas that the majority of the people never held or have long since abandoned. They continue trying to manipulate public opinion by the way they cover the news.

By exposing the errors and distortions of the media and the biases of those responsible, it is hoped that this book will help end this practice that is now a serious threat to one of the foundations of our democratic system.

ABC's "20/20" Is Toxic

How the TV program deceived the public

Victor Neufield, the executive producer of the ABC magazine program "20/20," says that he wants stories that are "hot" and "controversial." That was what he got with a program titled "The New Gold Rush" that aired on June 23, but producer Sharon Young and correspondent Lynn Sherr had to fiddle with the facts to come up with something that would meet the boss's craving for controversy.

Producer Sharon Young had obtained the cooperation of Newmont Gold Company in doing this segment by assuring its officials that she was interested in a "gold rush" story. Newmont is one of the pioneers in the mining of gold particles so small that they can only be seen through a microscope.

It's an interesting story revolving around technology, big investments and a shot in the arm for the economies of the areas in which the micro-gold is found. But that is not the kind of hot, controversial story that appeals to Mr. Neufield. When ABC News correspondent Lynn Sherr interviewed T. Peter Philip, the president of Newmont Gold Co., it was clear that her main interest wasn't in the gold rush. Her questions were almost all on the danger and threat that the new mines posed to human life, animal life and the physical environment. She also had questions about the big profits being made and why she wasn't getting a share of them, since many of the mines are on public land.

Jim Hill, Newmont's vice president for public affairs, had suspected that this might be the case, and he had taken the precaution of taping his talks with producer Sharon Young and had arranged to tape Sherr's interview of Mr. Philip. He had the tapes transcribed and provided the 50-page transcript to some 400 newspapers before the program aired so they

1

could compare what ABC had been told with what it actually reported.

The Elko (Nev.) *Independent* printed the entire transcript. It took up nine full columns in the paper, 143 column inches. The portions used on "20/20" took up three column inches. Mr. Philip and the other Newmont executives who gave ABC so much of their time had reason to feel deceived and cheated. But the viewers of the program were deceived and cheated even more. The Newmont officials had been lied to, but they knew it. The viewers were lied to, but few of them knew it.

The biggest danger that worried Sherr and her colleagues was the cyanide used by the mines to leach the gold out of the ore. Water containing 125 parts per million (ppm) of cyanide is sprayed over the crushed rock. The waste water ends up in ponds which, at the Newmont mines, have only 14-18 ppm of cyanide. Mr. Philip told Sherr that these were weak solutions and while they are toxic, they had caused no deaths or health problems. He explained the elaborate measures taken to guard against leaks from the ponds and to keep wildlife away from them. He said only two birds had been killed in their extensive string of ponds in seven months. He also told her that cyanide that might get into the ground would be broken down naturally by bacteria.

None of that fit the "20/20" script; none of it was used. Nor were anything but snippets of Mr. Philip's replies to questions Sherr had about the scarring of the landscape and the justification of the profits being made. Since Philip was the only person who appeared on the program to give the industry's side of the story, what the viewers got was an extremely unbalanced picture, heavily weighted in favor of environmentalist criticisms of mining operations.

The dishonest fiddling "20/20" did with the facts was most blatant in showing a man at both the beginning and the end of the program saying dramatically, "Would you drink cyanide? I sure don't want to, but I did." His well had been contaminated by a leak from a waste water pond at a mine in Montana. What "20/20" neglected to say was that the amount of cyanide found in his well was well below the ceiling that EPA is proposing for cyanide in drinking water. It

2

was perfectly safe, but the mine had provided him with a new well anyway. Co-host Barbara Walters and millions of viewers were fooled into thinking that the mine had endangered the life of this man and his family.

September 1, 1989

CUBAN DRUGS:
Where Are
The Media?

Why the American people know so little about Castro's drug trafficking to our country

This report concerns a major Cuban drug story you did not see on the national TV networks, nor read in your newspaper, unless you subscribe to *The Washington Times*. The afternoon of July 25 two former ranking Cuban officials testified at length to a House subcommittee concerning Fidel Castro's long involvement in drug smuggling. These two men, who chose freedom over life in Castro's police state, told how Castro set up bogus trading companies to smuggle dope. The hearing was open to the press and public, and reporters attended. Indeed, the reporter from *The Washington Post* wrote a long article, but one tacitly accepting Castro's current big lie about only recently having discovered drug activity in Cuba.

But the Post reporter ignored the Cubans' testimony. These were Oscar Valdes and Manuel de Beunza. Both men had big jobs in Cuba. Valdes, the brother of Ramiro Valdes, a politboro member, ran a private company in Canada which Castro created to evade the U. S. economic blockade. There were similar bogus firms in Panama and elsewhere. As Valdes testified, "Fidel saw in these firms the coverup he needed to organize his drug trafficking networks, because these companies were able to go around with impunity and were able to ship any merchandise to Cuba without anybody objecting."

The other witness, former counterintelligence officer de Beunza, told of a company called *Happy Line* which smuggled drugs via Panama. Castro's co-owner was Manuel Noriega, the Panamanian dictator. The Cubans who ran *Happy*

Line were ordered to "cooperate with drug smuggling operations," de Beunza testified.

This testimony came on the eve of Castro's 26th of July celebration marking the anniversary of the start of his revolution, and on the heels of the executions of four officers accused of drug smuggling. In fact, the witnesses said Castro was in the very midst of the smuggling rings in question. Given Castro's paranoia about ships and planes approaching Cuba from the U. S., he had to be aware of the vast traffic of cocaine and marijuana through his island. They reinforced the consensus of experts who believe Castro staged the show trial to rid himself of a potential political rival.

But the peculiar feature of the on-going drama in Cuba remains the failure of most of the U. S. media to go beyond Castro's big lie. In this instance, printed copies of the witnesses' testimony were distributed to the press, and the 52 pages contained explosive material about specifics of Castro's smuggling schemes. Yet *The New York Times*, *The Washington Post*, and the TV networks chose not to tell Americans about this important news.

Oscar Valdes does not seem surprised that Castro is getting away with his big lie. As a ranking Cuban official for years, he knows how skillfully Fidel Castro can manipulate the American media. As Valdes testified, "Castro always comes out with flying colors from all his endeavors, even with this denial of knowledge as to drug contraband." As long as a gullible media reports Castro's lies, and not the testimony of men who have fled his rule, an uninformed American public continues to be the prime victim.

August 10, 1989

Media Finance
One Side In
Child Care Debate

Why you seldom hear what's wrong with federalized day care

Conservatives have frequently complained that the major media are biased in favor of those demanding federalized day care. Actually, the situation is worse than commonly believed. One of the main groups promoting federal control of child care not only gets incredibly favorable publicity from the media, but is itself financed by major corporations and the media!

The Children's Defense Fund, the CDF, the six million dollar a year high-profile organization that has vigorously lobbied for Senator Christopher Dodd's controversial child care bill, boasts in its 1988 annual report of having received more than $50,000 in 1988 alone from *Exxon*. Other corporations or foundations that poured money into the CDF included the *Aetna Life and Casualty Foundation*, the *American Express Foundation*, the *AT&T Foundation*, the *General Mills Foundation*, the *Cummins Engine Foundation*, *General Motors*, *Mobil Oil*, *Xerox*, *Zayre*, *Sears* and *IBM*.

But it also received financial grants from *The Washington Post Company*, *Time Inc.*, and the *Discovery Cable Channel*, among others. The exact size of these donations was not disclosed. The annual report said only that they were under $10,000 each. Yet the *Post* did not disclose that it had any financial investment at all in the CDF when it ran a column on June 20 by Marian Wright Edelman, president of the Children's Defense Fund (CDF). The column was titled, *Pass That Child Care Bill*.

The CDF annual report says that its representatives met with editorial boards of major publications including *News-*

6

week, which is owned by the *Post, The Christian Science Monitor, The Boston Globe, The New York Times* and *The Atlanta Constitution.* On top of this, the foundations of the New York Times and *The Boston Globe* are listed in this same annual report as having given contributions of under $10,000 to the Children's Defense Fund. The CDF annual report also reveals that donations of over $500 were received from Jane Pauley, co-host of NBC's *Today* show, and her husband, cartoonist Garry Trudeau.

Interestingly, in boasting about its "national public education campaign" on behalf of federalized child care, the CDF says that its representatives appeared on several major news programs, including—surprise!—Jane Pauley's NBC *Today* show. But the *Today* show was not alone. On the subject of child care, the CDF says that it provided briefings for reporters and editorial boards that resulted "in more than 6,000 CDF-generated news stories and editorials, appearances on network and local television and radio programs, including ABC and CBS network news and the *Today* show . . ."

The CDF, a tax-exempt organization, claims it is non-partisan. Yet its much-ballyhood series of public service announcements on child care featured two prominent Democrats—Senate Majority Leader George Mitchell (Maine) and Jesse Jackson—and no Republicans. But please don't wait for the media to blow the whistle on that.

July 24, 1989

Quick to Smear, Slow to Clear

TV network bias exposed for all to hear

For three years the media had great sport baiting Lynn Nofziger, the bearded, rotund man who was Ronald Reagan's longtime political adviser. After leaving the White House Nofziger became a Washington lobbyist. And he soon found himself being prosecuted under the 1978 Ethics in Government Act, one of many post-Watergate laws.

When a jury convicted Nofziger in February 1988, all three networks gave him major story treatment in their lead segments. There were sketches by courtroom artists, sidewalk interviews with lawyers and an unrepentant Nofziger, and reproductions of the "smoking gun" documents said to have convinced jurors of his guilt. Tom Brokaw of NBC's *Nightly News* led into his story with a voice that sounded as if he was announcing a verdict from the judge's bench: "Nofziger . . . Guilty . . . Three Counts."

Peter Jennings of ABC's *World News Tonight* was not impressed when Nofziger said his conviction under what he called a "lousy law" was sort of like running a stop sign. Jennings said sternly, "Unless he wins on appeal, the law will send him to prison," emphasizing the severity of Nofziger's offense.

As it turns out, this particlar instance of what the networks liked to call "Reagan sleaze" did not survive an appeals court. In late June the D.C. Circuit Court of Appeals ruled that the law under which Nofziger was convicted was so ambiguous he could have not known his lobbying was illegal. The court found that there was no evidence that Nofziger had acted with criminal intent. But exoneration, in the networks' judgment, was not nearly so significant as conviction.

Conviction was the lead story; the reversal an also-mentioned item far down in the nightly newscasts. Dan Rather of the CBS *Evening News* set the general tone with his first sentence of a cursory report: "A setback for prosecutors on a key test of the ethics in government law today . . ."

Not a triumph for Nofziger after a legal struggle of almost three years, mind you, but defeat for the special prosecutor who had hounded him. Nofziger and his lawyers had a festive office party the afternoon of the verdict; according to the newspapers the former Reagan aide wore a Mickey Mouse tie to show his feelings about the law under which he was taken to court. This fete was a made-for-TV natural. But the cameras that had recorded Nofziger's disgrace were not present for his vindication: the networks used a mug shot imposed on the screens instead.

Roone Arledge, the president of ABC News, likes to brag about how the networks have surpassed newspapers as the most important source of news for the general public. His ABC, he boasts, is the prime source of news for more Americans than any other media outlet. But there is a serious flaw in the way ABC and the other networks do their business: it can be summarized as "Quick to smear . . . slow to clear."

July 13, 1989

Media
Still Unfair
to Quayle

Shocking details about dishonest reporting designed to hurt the Vice President

On May 24 United Press International carried a story on West Point commencement exercises stating that "boos and hisses arose from the corps of cadets" when Vice President Dan Quayle was introduced as the main speaker. Tom Brokaw referred to "boos and hisses" on the NBC *Nightly News* that evening, and *The Los Angeles Times* used the UPI story on its front page. Johnny Carson made Quayle the butt of several jokes on the NBC *Tonight Show*. Once again much of the media found occasion to ridicule the nation's vice president. But the UPI story had a major flaw: it was flat-out wrong.

The UPI story came from Michael O'Malley, of the Albany bureau, one of 72 media people accredited to the graduation. O'Malley, a four-year veteran of UPI, told us he heard "hisses" from undergraduates when the vice president was introduced. The story he dictated to his office mentioned "hisses" in the third or fourth paragraph. The story was relayed to UPI's main office in Washington, where O'Malley says a desk man "hyped it" by adding boos to the hisses, and making the supposed ridicule the lead paragraph. O'Malley was emphatic in stating he heard audible hisses.

If so, none of the 71 other reporters present did. Susan Bennett of the Knight-Ridder papers' Washington office, had in mind the campaign furor over Quayle's National Guard service, and wondered how the military crowd would receive him. "All of us there were looking for that very sort of thing if it did occur," Miss Bennett told us. "It simply did not happen—there was no hissing, no booing." She talked with many cadets and parents present; some liked Quayle, others

10

did not. But the general feeling was he had come to deliver a speech, and that what he said was well-received.

David Beckwith, a former *Time Magazine* reporter, now Quayle's press aide, heard of the UPI story shortly after his return to Washington at three in the afternoon. He hurriedly surveyed the six Washington-based reporters who had accompanied Quayle; none had heard boos or hisses. Nor could they be detected on a White House tape. By that time NBC News had already used the UPI story on a mid-afternoon *Newsbreak* narrated by Brokaw. CNN, which had a camera crew at West Point, ran two midday stories that did not mention jeering. Late in the afternoon, it did so, relying on UPI.

UPI, however, did not want to admit error, even after Beckwith invited its news executives to check with other reporters. Not until three hours of strong protests did UPI run a partial correction; this moved over UPI's wires around 5:30 p.m. Nonetheless, despite an alert, NBC *Nightly News* repeated the erroneous version that evening.

Lt. Gen. Dave R. Palmer, the West Point commandant, reminded UPI that a cadet who lies faces instant dismissal. He wrote, "No less a stringent standard should obtain among those who inform the American people than among those . . . sworn to defend them." UPI disagrees, for O'Malley still works there as a reporter.

June 28, 1989

CBS
Goes After
Bush

Evidence which shows CBS and Dan Rather are biased against the President

As President Bush anticipated his recent prime time news conference, he may have prepared extra hard for the questions asked by correspondents for CBS News. The reason: a new study has found that CBS News has been unusually critical of the Bush Administration during its first 100 days. The study was released by the Center for Media and Public Affairs in Washington, D.C. It found what it called striking and very unusual evidence relating to a difference of opinion among the networks on Bush's performance in office.

The center is run by Drs. Robert Lichter and Linda Lichter, co-authors with Professor Stanley Rothman of the book, *The Media Elite*. The book documents the liberal views held by many prominent journalists. Their study said that, "CBS has consistently rated Bush more poorly than the other two networks." It said that evaluations of Bush were only 39% positive on CBS, and that ratings of Bush's policies on the CBS *Evening News* ran 4 to 1 negative. However, it found that Bush was praised regularly on ABC, with positive evaluations 85% of the time, and evaluations of Bush on NBC were 63% positive.

As an example of CBS' negative coverage, the study cited a January 24 report by CBS News national affairs correspondent Lesley Stahl, who said, "(On) the budget deficit, (Bush) hit the ground walking . . . It's day two and there isn't even agreement on a format for budget talks." The study also noted that CBS News correspondent Wyatt Andrews complained about the Bush Administration's performance in a February 11th story that said Bush has "asked to rearrange national priorities but with a budget that doesn't rearrange them by much.''

Spokesmen for CBS News have not commented on the study. But another media watchdog group, the Media Research Center, has found similar results in its monitoring. On issue after issue, this group finds that the media, especially CBS, put Bush in the position of reacting to the Democratic party's agenda.

For example, on the issue of the budget deficit, the group finds that CBS News coverage has encouraged Bush to break his campaign pledge of "no new taxes" by raising them to bring in revenue. On the issue of the Exxon oil spill in Alaska, CBS News has suggested that Bush didn't move fast enough, that he didn't listen to the environmentalists, and that he didn't insist on enough government intervention. And on the proposal to raise the minimum wage, CBS News has suggested that Bush wasn't raising it enough.

The folks at Robert Lichter's Center for Media and Public Affairs say that such coverage doesn't necessarily suggest that CBS News is a liberal operation. They say that CBS News just has a different way of presenting the news. But the network is populated by Democrats. CBS News president David Burke served as an aide to several Democratic politicians, including Senator Ted Kennedy and former New York Governor Hugh Carey. And Dotty Lynch, CBS News political editor, worked for Democratic politicians such as former Senator Gary Hart and Senator Kennedy. Dan Rather himself is known to have a prejudice against Bush, if not Republicans in general.

June 23, 1989

PBS:
Lies About
My Lai

Another smear program about U.S. soldiers who fought in Vietnam

Some 14 years after the end of the Vietnam War, the Public Broadcasting System is still spending your tax dollars to berate the United States over Vietnam. PBS's latest smear was a *Frontline* documentary telecast on May 23 on the massacre of civilians in the village of My Lai in March 1969. The episode was horrible enough in true form, killings that sickened all Americans. Yet PBS distorted the historical record in its zeal to blacken America.

PBS's major error—and too big a one to be accidental—was its claim that the soldiers responsible for the massacre, Company C of the 11th Infantry Brigade, was a well trained and cohesive unit, men actually trained to kill innocent people. In fact, a formal Army inquiry headed by Lieutenant General W. R. Peers concluded that poor training was root cause of the troops going out of control. Peers noted that the brigade went to Vietnam a month early, "which meant cutting the final training period from eight to four weeks." Peer said, "Many of the men hardly knew one another, and there was a lack of cohesion in all the units." PBS, however, preferred to depict the men of Company C as trained killers typical of the entire American military.

PBS also did harm to the truth by using, in unquestioning form, the testimony of a My Lai veteran named Varnado Simpson. This man was obviously disturbed. Nine vials of pills were at his side during his interview, and he told of three suicide attempts. Simpson claimed that during his bloody day at My Lai he killed 20 to 25 people, and "cut their throats, cut off their hands, cut out their tongues, scalped them . . ."

14

We did not remember accounts of any such mutilations emerging during the many media and official inquiries into My Lai, so we did some checking. We found that Simpson had considerably amplified his story since he first spoke with NBC News and *The New York Times* in 1969. Then he admitted killing ten persons, not 20 to 25, and he said nothing about any mutilations. It took us less than half an hour to find these discrepancies. As a final check, we talked to F. Lee Bailey, the famed trial attorney who defended Captain Ernest Medina, one of the men tried for My Lai, and acquitted. Told of Simpson's mutilation claims, Bailey told us, "I doubt that it ever happened. We litigated the whole thing pretty thoroughly, and I'm sure it would have come to light."

Frontline worked on its documentary for months. Why did it not do the basic journalism involved in checking out Simpson's wild story? No one at the production company could give us an answer, although one man agreed that Simpson was a "pretty disturbed fellow." Nor would the *Frontline* press people make Simpson available to us for an interview about his conflicting stories.

These circumstances suggest that *Frontline* did not want the truth. Instead it wanted Simpson's gory testimony to enhance the drama on its American-bashing documentary. PBS in 1983 spent $5.6 million on a 13-part series *Vietnam: A Television History* which got rave reviews in Hanoi. So should its My Lai program.

June 8, 1989

Egg
On ABC's
Face

Fairness and accuracy as practiced at the TV network

At the annual shareholders meeting of CapCities/ABC last month, Chairman Tom Murphy boasted that more Americans receive their news from his network than from any other source. He paid special tribute to Roone Arledge, the president of ABC News, who, he said, would go down in broadcasting history for his accomplishments. Both those boasts may be true, but ABC News has had a big gob of egg on its face for over a year, and Roone Arledge has refused to wipe it off.

Twice last year, in April and May, ABC's *World News Tonight* featured charges made by an Oregon businessman named Richard Brenneke implicating a top aide to Vice President Bush in arms and drug smuggling deals. Brenneke had tried to interest the media in his story for months. He claimed that he had been involved in flying arms to the Nicaraguan freedom fighters and drugs into the U.S. He claimed that he took orders from Donald Gregg, who was Bush's national security adviser at the time.

Most journalists found that Brenneke's many stories did not hold water. He had been caught in too many contradictions and lies, including the claim that he had worked for the CIA for many years. But a couple of reporters decided to publicize his charges against Gregg. One was Richard Threlkeld of ABC, who put Brenneke on the air twice. The only other news organization that gave him any credence was *Newsweek Magazine*. Brenneke also gave a sworn deposition to a Senate subcommittee, headed by Senator John Kerry of Massachusetts, on the matter.

Accuracy in Media protested to ABC News about having

given Brenneke's charges nationwide publicity in view of his lack of credibility. We cited the evidence of his lies and contradictions, but ABC defended its tarnished source, offering the lame excuse that he had made the same charges in a sworn deposition for a Senate committee. ABC never explained why a sworn deposition by a proven liar should be given such credibility.

But even that weak excuse was discredited shortly before this year's annual ABC meeting. Senator Kerry issued a report in which he admitted that his staff had been unable to verify Brenneke's charges and they were therefore not included in his report. When Accuracy in Media representatives at the meeting insisted that ABC News owed Donald Gregg a correction and apology, Roone Arledge refused to acknowledge any such obligation. "The story is still out," he said.

Well, a significant part of the story came in a few weeks later. On May 25, a federal grand jury in Denver indicted Richard Brenneke for perjury for having lied under oath in making his wild charges against George Bush. Given ABC's unwillingness to admit that it had egg on its face over having given this liar such credence, it came as no surprise to us that Brenneke's indictment was not reported by ABC News. That would have been the decent, fair thing to do, providing an opportunity to correct the serious error made a year earlier. In refusing to wipe the egg off its face, ABC News is saying that it doesn't give high priority to fairness and accuracy.

June 7, 1989

Tutu
Out of
Touch

An example of why the American people are misinformed about South Africa

On May 17, Bryant Gumbel, host of NBC's *Today* show, talked with Randall Robinson, head of the lobbying group, TransAfrica, which is pushing for immediate black rule in South Africa. They discussed Archbishop Desmond Tutu, who was to meet later that day with President Bush. Robinson said Tutu intended to ask Bush for an immediate halt of all U.S. trade with South Africa. Gumbel ended the friendly conversation, which could not be called an interview, by bidding Robinson a cheery, "Good luck!"

Gumbel's attitude reflects the view that is common among American's black leaders, and our media, that they know what is best for the black people in South Africa. TransAfrica and other similar lobbying groups are pressuring American industry to abandon South Africa. They hope to create economic pressures that will force the white government to abandon its gradualist approach to integration and speed up the process.

The methods they and Archbishop Tutu advocate, do not reflect the wishes of South Africa's blacks. Bryant Gumbel did not ask Tutu about a poll that had just been released by the South African affiliate of Gallup International. Nor did he tell his audience anything about the findings of that poll on the issue of sanctions. Eighty-two percent of the 1400 blacks polled said that sanctions were a bad idea. Further, 85 percent of them oppose divestment by American firms of their holdings in South Africa.

Why do South African blacks differ from Archbishop Tutu on this? The poll showed that 55 percent rated unem-

18

ployment as one of the most serious problems facing South Africa compared to only 21 percent that cited apartheid. They realize that South Africa has the highest standard of living and the highest black per capita income of any African nation. The poll also found considerable support among blacks for the gradualist approach of the South African government. Sixty percent said they would oppose sanctions even if they believed they would force the resignation of the government within five years.

This very informative poll went almost unreported by our media. *The Washington Post* mentioned it briefly in two stories. The fact that South Africa's blacks overwhelmingly oppose sanctions is not considered newsworthy by our big media. Bishop Tutu, on the other hand, gets wonderful press in this country even though he obviously does not speak for South Africa's blacks.

The eagerness of our media to give the impression that Tutu is the foremost spokesman for South African blacks was demonstrated by the treatment he was given by ABC's *Nightline*. At the height of the student demonstration in China, Ted Koppel wanted to interview Tutu in preference to covering the Chinese students. He invited him to appear with two of his supporters and a sympathetic State Department official. The producer also invited the press secretary of the South African embassy to be on the program, saying, "We couldn't just stack the deck." He considered four to one to be balanced, but that was unacceptable to Tutu. He refused to appear, and Koppel, unwilling to discuss South Africa without Tutu, did his program on the Chinese demonstrations instead.

June 5, 1989

New Study
Indicts
The Media

The subtle way news people manipulate how you think

A new study finds that the major media are making liberal use of the word "conservative". The Media Research Center says that the major print media are continuing their "astonishing" practice of applying ideological labels in a manner that favors the left side of the political spectrum. The result of such bias is that readers of our major newspapers and news magazines receive a distorted view of news sources.

The study analyzed how reporters for the major print media over a two-year period used ideological tags in describing three groups or individuals on the right and left. The study was titled, "Looking for the Liberal Label". It says that labels are important because they enable the reader to consider the ideological slant of newsmakers' opinions, while the absence of labels can give a perception of objectivity and reliability.

The study found that the results show an astonishing contrast in the treatment of liberal and conservative organizations. Reporters labeled the conservative Heritage Foundation more than 35 times as often as the liberal Brookings Institution. *The New York Times*, for example, described Heritage as conservative, or a similar term, in 74 of 126 stories. This was an average of almost 60 percent. By contrast, in mentioning the Brookings Institution 271 times, the Times labeled it "liberal" only once.

The study also found that, "The conservative Concerned Women for America got tagged almost 20 times more frequently than the liberal National Organization for Women. On judicial issues, Ralph Neas, the liberal head of the Leadership Conference on Civil Rights, attracted less than a tenth of

20

the labels attached to the conservative Patrick McGuigan of the Free Congress Foundation." In total, the study found that the conservative groups and individuals were ideologically labeled an average of 58 percent of the time while the liberals were labeled only two percent of the time. The study covered the years 1987 and 1988 and was based on the use of the Nexis news data retrieval system. It included *The Washington Post, New York Times, Los Angeles Times, Newsweek, Time* and *U.S. News and World Report.*

Ideological labeling has always been a sore point with conservative critics of the media. Former *National Review* publisher William Rusher cited such a study when he spoke at the recent World Media Conference in Washington and charged that the major media are "dominated by a small group of people whose views are well to the left of the American majority." He noted that a study published in *Media Watch* years ago on how the media label certain politicians showed that conservative Senator Jesse Helms was labeled almost ten times as often as liberal Senator Edward Kennedy. In the case of Helms, Rush said, the media employed "warning references" such as "ultra right" or "arch conservative." Rusher charged that the media were busy slapping war paint all over Senator Helms while they were letting Senator Kennedy slip by. It's no surprise that Rusher's speech to the World Media Conference got no coverage from the liberal media.

May 23, 1989

New York Times Smears Freedom Fighters

How a newspaper can mislead its readers

The *New York Times* has been accused of publishing fabrications and unsubstantiated allegations against the anticommunist Angolan movement, UNITA, the Union for the Total Independence of Angola. UNITA is a group of freedom fighters under the leadership of Angolan nationalist leader, Dr. Jonas Savimbi, which has been engaged for more than ten years in a guerrilla struggle against a Communist regime.

The Times published extremely damaging stories about UNITA and Savimbi on March 11 and 12 under sensational headlines saying that ex-allies of UNITA claimed that the group had tortured and murdered dissenters within the organization.

Fred Bridgland, the author of a sympathetic biography of Savimbi, was reported as the main source of some of the most damaging allegations.

But in a letter to the Times, Bridgland said the paper used him as a source in such a way as to have "wildly overstepped the bounds of journalistic ethics." He said, "I specifically refused to speak to *The New York Times* because I believe reporting of the Angola crisis in your paper has been consistently skewed . . . I was put under pressure by your journalists and finally agreed to talk to them off the record. That was the solemn agreement, and I trusted it. To have broken that pledge is regrettable."

Bridgland also went on to say that, "what is truly objectionable is to see statements and convictions attributed to me which I have simply not subscribed to. Most of them are fabrications." Contrary to what the Times reported, Bridgland said he did not say that Tito Chingunji, until recently

UNITA's Washington-based foreign secretary, had been tortured. Bridgland also denied that he had any association, as reported in the Times, with a group of UNITA students in Sweden who claim that former UNITA officials have been put under house arrest or murdered. Bridgland said he has never met with those students or voiced those opinions.

More doubt about the Times stories has been raised by Congressman Dan Burton, the vice chairman of the House Subcommittee on African Affairs. Burton, who led a delegation to Angola in February, told a recent news conference that he was shocked by the Times stories, written by correspondents in London and Washington, D. C., because they contradicted what he and others had seen firsthand.

He said *The New York Times* had a reporter, Christopher Wren, in Angola ,"when we were there and he saw everything we saw. But all of their reporting on this story has come from Europe and Washington. That doesn't make sense to me." Getting down to specifics, Burton said he met with UNITA deputy secretary Tito Chingunji, whom *The New York Times* reported to be tortured or under house arrest, and found him to be in good health. The Times also reported that UNITA General Tony Fernandes was nearly beaten to death seven years ago. But Burton said his delegation was briefed by General Fernandes in Washington before the trip and the general is still a member and supporter of UNITA. The Times just about got everything wrong.

April 28, 1989

60 Minutes
Is Dangerous
To Health

The grossly false report on Alar-sprayed apples

60 Minutes is a powerful program. It reaches an audience of millions and it can be very persuasive. That was proven when it aired a frightening report on February 26 about the alleged danger of children's health lurking in apples and apple products.

Correspondent Ed Bradley began the program with this ominous statement: "The most potent cancer-causing agent in our food supply is a substance sprayed on the apples to keep them on the trees longer and make them look better. That's the conclusion of a number of scientific experts, and who is most at risk? Children who may some day develop cancer from this one chemical called daminozide."

Mr. Bradley went on to say that the cancer risk to children from drinking juice made from apples treated with this chemical "is perilously high." He suggested that the Environmental Protection Agency was endangering the health of millions of children by not banning the use of daminozide instantly. He claimed that the Food and Drug Administration was negligent in permitting apple products to be sold that contain dangerously high levels of the pesticide. The program ended up telling parents that there is no way they can be sure that apple products they buy in the supermarket don't contain dangerous levels of daminozide or another chemical formed when it is heated, UDMH.

These frightening charges were promptly reported in the press and were the topic of discussion on other television and radio talk shows. *The Donahue Show*, which is viewed by millions of housewives, weighed in with a one-sided discussion stressing the dangers of apples that featured actress

24

Meryl Streep. During the show, one alarmed mother in the audience asked where she could take her child to have him tested for cancer. Mothers around the country were reported to be taking apple juice off the shelf and pouring it down the drain.

Already several school systems including New York, San Francisco, Los Angeles and Fairfax county in Virginia have announced that they were pulling apples from school cafeterias because of the concerns generated by these charges. A survey done by the Wirthlin Group found that 62 percent of those polled said they had heard or read something recently that made them think that apples are unsafe. Four out of ten specifically mentioned reports linking apples to pesticides that cause cancer. A fourth of those surveyed said they were going to stop eating apples or cut down their consumption.

Apple producers, processors, the EPA, and the Food and Drug Administration and many scientists around the country were very unhappy, even angry, about these reports, and they had good reason to be. *60 Minutes*, Mr. Donahue and the other scaremongers had seized on a sensational report put out by a liberal environmental group called the Natural Resources Defense Council that was based on faulty data that gave a wildy exaggerated account of the risks posed by daminozide.

Mr. Bradley's opening statement, made against a graphic showing a big red apple with a skull and crossbones on it, was false, according to Bruce Ames. Mr. Ames is the famed University of California biochemist who, with Dr. Lois Gold, devised a widely used test to measure the cancer-causing potential of various substances. They rate daminozide and its derivative, UDMH, below chlorine-treated tap water as a carcinogenic risk. Giving tap water a value of 1.0, they rate peanut butter at 30, beer at 2,800, and daminozide plus UDMH at under 1.0. That means that daminozide poses about the same risk as tap water and that peanut butter poses 30 times the risk of both of them.

The EPA has stated that the NRDC's estimates of the risk posed by pesticide residue in food, including apple products, are "far out of line with existing data." It had announced its decision to proceed with canceling the registration of daminozide as an approved pesticide on February 1, on the ground that it poses some health risk, but not enough to justify treating it as an imminent hazard. It assures the public that food containing pesticide residues within the legal limits are safe for people of all ages.

The National Research Council and the National Academy of Sciences recently issued a lengthy report advising Americans to double their consumption of fruits and vegetables. It said that while this would result in higher intake of pesticide residues, the potential increase risk would be greatly outweighed by the increased benefits from reduced risk of cancer and other chronic diseases brought about by a healthier diet. *60 Minutes*, in scaring the public about apples and other fruits and vegetables, probably did far more harm to people's health than the pesticides it was attacking.

If CBS were really concerned about our health, it would promptly have *60 Minutes* do a segment putting the pesticide/daminozide issue in proper perspective, using up-to-date information. They should interview scientists such as Bruce Ames who don't accept the notion that any chemical that causes cancer in mice must be banned, even though it may be far less carcinogenic than common foods such as peanut butter.

March 10, 1989

Moral Bankruptcy at CBS

The network flouts its promises to be fair and accurate

CBS and the producers of *60 Minutes* have shown themselves to be morally bankrupt. For weeks, Don Hewitt, the executive producer of *60 Minutes*, gave assurances that they were going to do a second program on Alar and apples that would be fair. That would have been in sharp contrast to the one-sided program aired on February 26 that set off the great apple scare, costing apple growers and processors an estimated $100 million in lost sales. At the CBS annual shareholders meeting on May 10, we criticized the decision to put David Gelber, the producer of the first program, in charge of the follow-up. He would naturally try to vindicate himself.

Howard Stringer, president of CBS Broadcast Group, defended this decision, saying Gelber had a long reputation for fairness. He promised that the second program would be "fair and accurate in the grand tradition of *60 Minutes*". That is what we were afraid of. The first *60 Minutes* program had claimed Alar was "the most potent cancer-causing agent in our food supply," ignoring a recent finding that rodent tests of Alar had turned out negative for cancer. Challenged to defend the fairness and accuracy of that, Howard Stringer replied, "I think *60 Minutes* on Sunday [will] answer those questions . . . and reassure the public." Laurence Tisch, the president of CBS, added, "CBS has only one obligation—to broadcast something that's fair. And we will carry out that obligation."

When the program aired on May 14 it made liars out of Laurence Tisch, Howard Stringer and Don Hewitt. As we feared, producer David Gelber ran roughshod over accuracy and fairness in his effort to vindicate his first program. Even

27

though the CBS News operating standards require that significant errors of fact be corrected promptly and fully, *60 Minutes* failed to acknowledge or correct the most serious factual error made in its first program—the statement that Alar is the most potent cancer-causing agent in our food supply.

Flouting the promises to be fair and accurate, CBS not only failed to mention that the latest tests had shown that Alar didn't cause cancer in rodents, but it actually referred to Alar as a carcinogen or possible carcinogen ten times in that second program that was supposed to reassure the public. They had an opportunity to tell the public that Alar-treated raw apples contain no carcinogen and should not be shunned by even those fearful of even minute traces of cancer-causing chemicals. Having caused growers, who are stuck with millions of perfectly wholesome apples, huge financial losses, that was the least CBS could have done. The nearest it came to doing so was in this reminder by correspondent Ed Bradley: "Remember, there's more concern about Alar in juice than in raw apples because there's more of the dangerous breakdown product, UDMH." He didn't mention that this is because UDMH is formed when Alar-treated apples are heated to make juice. Even in the juice, the amount of UDMH is so infinitesimal that Consumers Union has not tested for it, explaining that the tests are too costly and complicated. In other words, it is to all intents and purposes undetectable, but it is assumed to be there.

The first *60 Minutes* program on apples was criticized severely for having accepted the premise that infinitesimal traces of carcinogenic chemicals in our food supply are a serious problem. They promised to give the opposing view a hearing in their second program. One of the country's top biochemists and an expert on carcinogens, Dr. Bruce Ames, chairman of the biochemistry department of the University of California, Berkeley, was interviewed. Ames likes to point out that the risks of getting cancer from eating such wholesome foods as peanut butter, mushrooms and celery is far greater than the risk from drinking apple juice. He says that all plants produce their own pesticides for self-protection and that tests show about half of them are carcinogenic. He says

28

our food contains far more of these natural carcinogens than man-made carcinogenic chemical residues. There is no evidence that either of them are a cause of cancer in man and that we should worry about them.

Ames, the winner of the country's most prestigious award for cancer research and the highest award in environmental achievement, has an international reputation. *60 Minutes* put him on the air very briefly, but they tried to diminish his credibility every way possible. They didn't mention his impressive credentials. They said he had been urged upon them by the agricultural chemical industry, not mentioning others who had recommended him. They tried to rebut or discredit what he said, using a chemist who was falsely identified as heading a laboratory at the National Cancer Institute. The man is employed by a company with an NCI contract, and he is not authorized to speak for NCI. He is known as a radical environmentalist, but CBS didn't mention that. Nor did they say who urged that he be interviewed. He was put on to challenge Dr. Ames, but Ames was given no opportunity to reply or challenge him.

That is fairness and accuracy in the grand tradition of *60 Minutes*.

May 19, 1989

CBS Blamed
For Jailing of
Freedom Fighter

Innocent man goes to Nicaragua jail because of the program West 57th

John Hull, an American supporter of the Nicaraguan Freedom Fighters, is blaming falsehoods aired on CBS News' *West Fifty-Seventh* for his recent jailing by Costa Rican authorities on charges of drug smuggling. The 68 year old American, for decades, has run a ranch in Costa Rica. Because of his assistance to the Nicaraguan resistance, Hull has been an ongoing target of the Sandinista government and its supporters, as well as media figures trying to discredit U.S. attempts to establish democracy in Central America.

Hull, who is both diabetic and suffers from a heart ailment, was imprisoned from January 12 through March 10 under arduous conditions that he says threatened his life. The charges were that he was part of a CIA-controlled network shipping arms into Costa Rica for the Freedom Fighters, and smuggling narcotics back into the United States to raise money to buy more weapons.

But according to Hull, the bogus charges did not result from any independent investigation by the Costa Rican authorities. Instead, Hull told Arthur Randall of the *Washington Inquirer*, "the actual charges state on their face" that they were based on allegations made on a *West Fifty-Seventh* segment aired April 6, 1987. The Costa Rican police, Hull told Randall, tried to coerce him into signing a "confession" that would implicate not only former Marine Colonel Oliver North, but Ronald Reagan and George Bush as well, in the supposed drug scheme.

The producer of the *West Fifty-Seventh* segment on John Hull was Leslie Cockburn, author of a book on Central

America entitled *Out of Control*. Some of Cockburn's information, she states in the book, came from the discredited left-wing Christic Institute of Washington. A Christic Institute lawsuit charging that a "secret team" of retired military men and intelligence officers ran a covert American foreign policy for years was recently thrown out of court as baseless. The charges against Hull that Cockburn used in her broadcast were similar to ones in the Christic lawsuit.

Hull, in his interview with Randall, accused left-wing supporters of Oscar Arias, the Costa Rican president, of arresting him on the trumped up charges in the hope he would die in jail. He was denied medical treatment and food during his ordeal and survived only because of sympathetic fellow prisoners who resent the increasingly pro-communist stands of the Arias government.

Author Leslie Cockburn, meanwhile, faces continuing problems with her book *Out of Control*. Retired Major General Richard V. Secord, one of the men she and the Christics accused of being part of the "secret team," is suing her for libel. Secord's lawyers are taking depositions from Cockburn in April during which they intend to press her to name the sources of the many wild allegations she made against Freedom Fighter supporters in her book. The ordeal of John Hull, meanwhile, is graphic evidence of the results of the McCarthyite Christic vendetta against freedom fighters—a smear campaign assisted by Leslie Cockburn and CBS News.

April 21, 1989

Can The Media Cope With Science?

How one-sided news reporting helped kill a nuclear power plant

Dr. Bernard Cohen, one of our leading nuclear physicists, says that the U. S. government's science and technology policies are being guided by "emotion-driven public opinion rather than by sound scientific advice." For over a decade, Dr. Cohen has labored to try to get journalists to understand and communicate the fact that nuclear power is not the great threat to health and safety that it has been portrayed to be. He and other nuclear scientists have watched in dismay as politicians in New York and Massachusetts have kept nuclear power plants costing in excess of $5 billion each from being put into service because of irrational fears instilled by anti-nuclear fear mongers.

Even before the disgraceful drama of Shoreham and Seabrook nuclear power plants had played out, Dr. Cohen in 1984 wrote, "Unfortunately, this public opinion is controlled by the media, a group of scientific illiterates, drunk with power, heavily influenced by irrelevant political ideologies, and so misguided as to believe that they are more capable than the scientific community of making scientific decisions." He warned that unless something was done about this, he feared the United States would become an impoverished nation within the next century.

Nothing has been done about it in the last five years, and the situation is getting worse. While other countries are solving the energy crises and pollution crises of the future by pushing ahead with new nuclear power plants, we are on the verge of destroying the completed but unused Shoreham plant

32

on Long Island without letting it generate a kilowatt of the power that area so badly needs.

This has been too much for the editorial board of *The New York Times*, which has belatedly condemned those blocking the operation of Shoreham as "energy vandals." A Times editorial points out that Shoreham would save more than eight million barrels of oil a year, that it would combat the feared warming of our atmosphere from the burning of fossil fuels (the greenhouse effect), that it would help solve the acid rain problem and would reduce dependence on imports of foreign oil. The Times points out that the risks of nuclear power plants have been "vastly exaggerated."

The Times asks, "Who is to blame for the historic folly of scrapping Shoreham?" It blames the people of Long Island, who, it says, have "punished any politician who dared tell them the truth." It blames Gov. Mario Cuomo, who "joined the fear-mongers" instead of educating the public. It blames the president of the Long Island Lighting Co., the owner of Shoreham, for not being sufficiently vigorous in fighting "the dragon Long Islanders had created." It blames the Nuclear Regulatory Commission and the New York State Legislature, who lacked the courage to do what was necessary to save the plant.

Missing from this long list of the culpable is any mention of Prof. Bernard Cohen's prime target, the media, including *The New York Times* itself. While the Times has been running editorials for several years in favor of letting Shoreham operate, its news stories have tended to be overwhelmingly negative about nuclear power. Herbert Jaffe, a public spirited Long Islander who has done battle for the nuclear power plant, says his neighbors are making the blunder of scrapping the plant "because no responsible source has given them the information they need to make an informed decision." He says to the Times, "Don't blame the politicians. They have to run for election. You don't."

Jaffe has pointed out that the opponents of the plant have been making use of a fake cancer survey that purported to show that the 1979 nuclear accident at Three Mile Island in 1979 had resulted in an increased incidence of cancer. He said he provided *New York Times* reporters with copies of the report by the Pennsylvania State Board of Health exposing the fake survey. They made no use of it. He says the New York State Energy Office used fake electricity demand projections in its battle to justify scrapping Shoreham. He says The Times didn't expose that either. *Newsday*, the Long Island paper, has been even worse, and TV has joined in sinking Shoreham.

April 20, 1989

Networks
Ignore Lesson
of Afghanistan

*American TV coverage favors the Communist aggressors
who killed one million Afghans*

The Soviets ended their nine year occupation of Afghanistan on February 15th. It is estimated that more than one million Afghans died and five million fled their country. But the
bitter lesson of Afghanistan—that freedom from communism
had been purchased only with great suffering and loss of
life—was not the lesson that two television networks, CBS
and CNN, relayed in their coverage of the Soviet withdrawal
from that country.

That's the conclusion of a new study by *Media Watch*,
published by the Media Research Center. It has given its
March 1989 "Janet Cooke Award" to CNN and CBS for
ignoring the atrocities and brutal nature of the occupation of
Afghanistan in stories leading up to the Soviet pullout. The
award, given to distinguish the most outrageously distorted
news story of the month, is named for the former *Washington
Post* reporter who got caught fabricating a story.

The finding regarding CBS was surprising because CBS
has been anti-Soviet in its coverage of Afghanistan over the
years. CBS was the only network, for example, that aired a
prime-time documentary on the conflict, and CBS *Evening
News* anchorman Dan Rather himself did one of the initial
television reports about the war from inside Afghanistan.

But the new study finds that, "CBS and CNN spent much
of their airtime looking upon the Soviet occupation uncriti-
cally while impugning the freedom fighters" in the weeks
preceding the Soviet withdrawal. The study says, "While the
Soviets had engaged in weeks of saturation bombing and
offenses against civilian villages before their pullout, just four

35

of 14 CBS stories made any reference to these offenses. But plenty of time was given to supposed 'rebel' indiscretions.'' The study found that the same pattern held for CNN. It found that only seven of 38 stories by correspondents or summaries by anchors made any reference to Soviet atrocities.

CBS News reporter Barry Petersen was criticized for a January 31st report that showed film footage of Afghan resistance fighters executing government soldiers and which concluded, ''Afghan soldiers will face a situation as brutal as any the Soviets are leaving behind. . . Many fear this is just a taste of what is to come once the Soviets are gone.'' The study was particularly critical of CNN Moscow bureau chief Steve Hurst, charging that he lent legitimacy to the Soviet invasion with a January 27th report that it was ''instigated partly out of fear'' of fundamentalism on the border of the Soviet Union. On February 9, Hurst reported that the fall of the Marxist regime would be detrimental to women's rights in a report that claimed, ''It's the women of this country who have the most to lose if this Marxist revolution fails—if the government falls to the fundamentalist Moslem rebels.''

The study said the apparent bias against the resistance in some of the reports stemmed from where they were broadcast from. All of Hurst's stories, the publication said, originated from communist-controlled territory in Afghanistan. CBS, it said, did much the same.

April 12, 1989

Dan Rather's Nemesis Speaks Out

A behind-the-camera view of the infamous attack on George Bush

The chief media advisor to George Bush's presidential campaign, who once denounced Dan Rather of CBS News as "the most biased reporter in the history of broadcasting," said recently that "the secret" to ensuring fair coverage is for the public "to stay involved in public information" by pressuring networks and advertisers. Roger Ailes, regarded as the mastermind behind Bush's successful media appearances and advertising campaign, said that people should follow the lead of Terry Rakolta, the Michigan housewife and mother whose letter writing campaign against gratuitous sex on a Fox Television program prompted several major companies to drop their advertising on it.

Ailes said the same tactics can work to change news programs for the better. "If they write letters to the network," he said, "that tends to steer things in the right direction." Ailes said that he has already noticed a change in the CBS *Evening News*, long regarded by conservatives and media critics as the most liberal of the three networks. He said, "I think Dan (Rather) has been meticulously fair since the election," but quickly added, "I don't know what has brought that about."

Ailes made his comments after his appearance on a panel at the World Media Conference, where he discussed the media and the electoral process. One of the matters he discussed was Dan Rather's now-famous January 25, 1988, interview of then-vice president and candidate George Bush on the CBS *Evening News*. The interview, which concerned Bush's role in the Iran arms affair, was preceded by a taped report exposing what was purported to be Bush's lies and eva-

37

sions on the subject. During the interview, Rather repeatedly interrupted Bush, telling him at one point that the Reagan Administration's Iran policy "made us hypocrites in the eyes of the world." At the end of the interview, Bush was abruptly cut off by Rather.

Rather's conduct, a violation of CBS News guidelines requiring fairness and objectivity, was strongly criticized within the journalism profession and by the public, which bombarded CBS and its affiliates with angry letters and phone calls.

Ailes said, "I was with the vice president when he had his debate with Dan Rather. CBS hired a Democratic consultant to coach Dan Rather over the weekend on how he should debate the vice president. CBS News spent a hundred thousand dollars putting together a five minute piece to indict the vice president. And Dan Rather's job was to convict him and execute him on the air."

Ailes said it was interesting to note that the consultant for Dan Rather in that event later worked for Michael Dukakis. Ailes said that when he walked up on stage for the final presidential debate in Los Angeles, he and Bush looked across the stage and saw that the handler for Rather was now the handler for Dukakis. "We thought that was somewhat amusing," Ailes said. "I thought it more amusing than the vice president did." The Democratic consultant involved in the Rather interview and the Dukakis campaign was identified by Ailes as Tom Donilon, who has a history of involvement in Democratic party politics.

April 10, 1989

FLAG BURNING:
A One-Sided
CBS View

Only those in favor of flag burning appear on CBS

The day before the U.S. Supreme Court heard a case on whether burning the American flag is "freedom of speech" or desecration of a national symbol, CBS *This Morning* gave a forum to three radicals who took the predictable position: that torching Old Glory is not vandalism, but an act of political protest protected by the First Amendment of the U.S. Constitution. The CBS presentation excluded such persons as veterans who fought to defend the flag and what it symbolizes. Instead, the three America-bashers were given free vocal rein by co-host Harry Smith.

The case involves Gregory Johnson, a member of the Revolutionary Communist Youth Brigade, who burned a flag during a demonstration at the 1984 Republican National Convention in Dallas. He was convicted of violating a state law against desecration and sentenced to a year in jail and a $2,000 fine. The Texas Court of Criminal Appeals reversed the conviction on grounds that the law under which Johnson was convicted was overly broad. But the State of Texas appealed the dismissal to the Supreme Court, arguing that the flag is "this nation's cherished property." As a Dallas assistant district attorney told the court, "We're asking respect for the flag's physical integrity."

But the Dallas prosecutor and other Americans who revere the flag received no hearing on CBS *This Morning*. Instead, Harry Smith put on defendant Gregory Johnson, his attorney, the long-time radical William Kuntzler, and a Chicago art student named Dredd Scott Tyler. The latter recently staged a photomontage at the Chicago Art Institute titled "What is the Proper Way to Display the American Flag?" featuring photos

39

of flags being burned. Tyler put an American flag on the floor and invited viewers to stand on it and write their comments in a book. Outraged veterans from the VFW and other groups staged a protest of their own and tried to shut down Tyler's "show." The U.S. Senate unanimously passed a bill barring such disrespectful display of the flag.

In the CBS segment interviewer Smith listened impassively as the radicals savaged the flag as a symbol of oppression which they claimed is hated worldwide. The interviews came in the midst of demonstrations supporting flag-burning sponsored by the Revolutionary Communist Youth Brigade outside the Supreme Court and elsewhere. Literature distributed at the court rally urged sympathizers to stir up media atention. The literature listed as supporting groups such groups as the Christic Institute, The American Civil Liberties Union, and People for the American Way.

The Christic Institute, which recently lost its suit charging that a "secret team" ran U.S. foreign policy, also filed an amicus brief with the Supreme Court supporting flag-burning. Punishing someone for burning a flag, the Christics said, would "sound a death knell for any meaningful concept of justice in this land." Brave people died defending a flag that symbolizes the right of free speech, but CBS *This Morning* didn't permit a voice to be heard in its defense.

April 6, 1989

"Dirty Tricks"
By
PBS

*Another smear-America program on the Public
Broadcasting Service*

The Public Broadcasting Service (PBS) finished airing a
four-hour series condemning the use of covert action by U.S.
intelligence agencies in mid-February. For four hours, Bill
Kurtis, the former co-host of the CBS *Morning News* program, reviewed what he portrayed as the futility and folly of
American efforts to try to achieve our foreign policy objectives by using covert action, sometimes labeled "dirty
tricks," against our enemies. To make his case, Kurtis went
back 35 years to review covert CIA operations in Iran and
Guatemala in 1953. These have long been considered good
examples of successful covert actions, but Kurtis presented
them as both wicked and as failures.

They were portrayed as wicked because the producers
didn't think the United States had any business intervening to
keep Third World countries from falling under the control of
the Soviet Union, a country highly skilled in using covert
action to extend its influence and control. They were portrayed as failures because neither Iran nor Guatemala had
ended up with perfect governments and lived happily ever
after.

To make that case, PBS distorted the facts surrounding
the CIA-backed coups. It also jumped to the totally unwar-
ranted conclusion that anything bad that had happened in Iran
and Guatemala since 1953, including the rise of the Ayatollah
Khomeini, could be blamed on those coups. What might have
happened if we had let both Iran and Guatemala fall under
Soviet influence or control in 1953 was not discussed.

The PBS series didn't try to provide any perspective by

41

showing what had happened to the countries that have fallen under Soviet influence or control during the last 35 years. It's a long list: Cuba, Vietnam, Cambodia, Laos, Ehtiopia, Angola, Mozambique, Nicaragua, and Afghanistan, to cite those that are best known. In some cases the United States tried and failed to keep the country from falling to the communists, using both covert intelligence actions and military force. In others, we tried to help their oppressed people free themselves. In still others, we did nothing.

Our successes may not have ushered in a millennium of paradise in the countries we tried to help, but our failures have in every case resulted in unending hell for those who fell under the yoke of communism. Communism in the Third World has meant bloodbaths, boat people, masses of political prisoners, millions of refugess, loss of freedom, impoverishment, and war. The PBS series never discussed that.

Ironically, this smear on America's efforts to prevent these disasters was airing while the Soviet army of invasion was withdrawing from Afghanistan. Nine years ago, few held any hope that the Afghan guerrillas, the mujahideen, would be successful in resisting the mighty Red Army. Thanks to the help provided covertly by "America's secret army of intervention," as Bill Kurtis labeled the CIA, the mujahideen won a historic victory. The PBS series took no notice. That didn't fit their blame-America scenario. PBS was more interested in its own "dirty tricks" than in presenting an intelligent program about intelligence.

March 11, 1989

The
Real
Dan Rather

A case where the newsman's bias hung out for all to hear

In a recent interview with *The New York Times*, former CBS anchorman Walter Cronkite said, "All through my life I have never disguised my sentiments about politics in general. . . liberalism came out in almost every speech, in one way or another, on radio." Recognizing that this admission could call into question the objectivity of CBS News, he added, "On television, I tried absolutely to hew to the middle of the road and not show any prejudice or bias in any way." It is not true that Walter Cronkite's reporting on television was never colored by his strong liberal views, but his bias was admittedly more apparent in his commentaries on CBS radio.

That is a tradition that his successor, Dan Rather, has continued. Like Cronkite, Rather's reporting on the *CBS Evening News* often reflects his liberal bias. His notorious ambush interview of Vice President Bush on the eve of the Iowa caucuses in January 1988 in which he tried to derail Bush's campaign for the presidency was a prize example of partisanship in the news. But following in Cronkite's footsteps, Rather is even less restrained in the daily radio broadcast aired by CBS News under the title, *Dan Rather Reporting*.

As the trial of Col. Oliver North got underway in Washington last month, Dan Rather used his radio program to spread his suspicion that Reagan and Bush wanted to cover up the truth about the Iran arms affair. In his reports on the legal maneuvering that was going on at the beginning of the trial over the handling of classified documents, Rather delivered some very harsh comments about what he suggested were efforts by the Bush administration to cover up the truth.

The trial was delayed for several days while Attorney

43

General Richard Thornburg tried to work out procedures to safeguard highly classified material North's attorneys said they needed to defend their client properly. Congress has spelled out the procedures to be followed in such cases. It made the Attorney General responsible for protecting classified material.

Rather should have known this, but he told his listeners this was part of "extraordinary efforts at some of the highest levels to stop the North trial." He flatly accused President Bush and Attorney General Thornburg of "working" to keep the North case from going before a jury. He asked, "Are THEY trying to get for Oliver North a de facto pardon?" He identified the THEY as the people he said had been working long and hard to cover up what had happened in the Iran arms affair.

Rather's suspicions were baseless. The procedures for handling the classified documents were agreed upon and the trial got underway. Even the very liberal *New York Times* columnist Anthony Lewis, who is no friend of the Bush Administration, said the cynical view that had been broadcast by Dan Rather was "totally rejected by those who know the most about the case." Lewis said he was not aware of any lawyer on either side who thought Thornburg was "acting for political reasons or in anything but good faith." Rather had not been reporting what knowledgeable experts thought. He had simply been giving vent to his own liberally biased judgment.

March 9, 1989

The Leak
That
Backfired

Famed reporter Bob Woodward favors "Holy s--t" story to the truth

Bob Woodward, the famed investigative reporter-editor of *The Washington Post*, ended up with egg on his face when he and his editors bit on a story fed to them by a Senate source "involved in the Tower nomination process." The source appeared to be responding to a Post editorial on February 28 saying that Sen. Sam Nunn, the leader of the opposition to John G. Tower's confirmation as Secretary of Defense, should spell out specifically what he found in Tower's record that caused him to oppose the nomination.

On March 2, the day the debate on Tower's nomination began in the Senate, there appeared on the front page of the Post the leaked story under Woodward's byline headlined: "Incidents at Defense Base Cited, Drunkenness, Harassment of Women Alleged." "Informed sources" had told Woodward that "one section of the material on Tower that has attracted the attention of senators . . . concerns two visits Tower made to Bergstrom Air Force Base in Austin, Texas, in 1976-78, when he allegedly appeared to be drunk and fondled two women."

This charge had been made in a letter to Sen. Nunn by retired Air Force sergeant Bob Jackson, who claimed to have observed both incidents. Jackson had claimed that during both visits to the base, Tower "had liquor on his breath and he had trouble talking and was staggering out of the car and up the steps." He reported that Sen. Tower had put his hand on the breast of a secretary, "who drew back and said nothing." In the other incident, Jackson said that Tower had put his hand on the shoulder of a female crew chief and that "it traveled

45

down and rested on her rump for a short period of time." He claimed that three or four other military personnel had witnessed both incidents.

Woodward confirmed that Jackson had made these charges, but even though he claims that he always insists on two sources for a story, he ran with this one without locating any of the other alleged witnesses. His rigorous test was apparently satisfied when Jackson told him that an FBI agent who interviewed him had told him that the FBI had another witness who had corroborated his story. It didn't seem to trouble him that the FBI had not included Jackson's claims in its thick report on John Tower, nor, as he noted in his story, had the bureau reported these charges to the White House.

In what appeared to be a direct response to the Post's editorial challenge to Sen. Nunn, Woodward said that the fact that the senators knew of the Jackson story and the White House did not "may in part explain some of the different reactions to the nomination." He wrote: "President Bush and leading Republicans have said they have seen nothing that would disqualify (Tower), while leading Democrats, including Nunn, maintain that the investigations show a pattern of bad judgment that renders him unfit for the sensitive post."

If this was indeed intended as an answer to that Post editorial, it backfired badly. An investigation that should have been made before this charge was made public disclosed that the only visit Sen. Tower had made to Bergstrom Air Force Base was in 1975. Sgt. Jackson was not assigned to the base until 1976. Three witnesses, including the base commander and the sergeant assigned to escort dignitaries at the time of Tower's visit, all say that Tower behaved perfectly properly. Tower's accuser, Sgt. Jackson, was diagnosed in 1977, as having "symptoms of a mixed personality disorder with anti-social themes and hysterical features." He was found unable to perform his duties and was retired from the Air Force in 1978.

These facts were laid out at a press conference by Sen. John McCain and others only hours after *The Washington Post* story was published. Sen. William S. Cohen, (R.-Maine), said that the Armed Services Committee had given no serious consideration to Jackson's charges because of "the lack of credible, corroborating evidence." He said he was surprised to see it in *The Washington Post*. Sen. Nunn was quoted in the Post the next day as saying that Jackson's story "was merely one item which was cumulative of other information about Sen. Tower's excessive drinking in the 1970's ... Therefore, this item was not a significant factor in my own thoughts, or I believe, in the committee's deliberations."

To its credit, *The Washington Post* published a front-page story on March 3, giving the facts divulged by the Republican senators, but that didn't undo all the damage that had been done to Senator Tower's reputation. The person whose reputation should suffer from this is Bob Woodward, who has once again shown that he prefers what he calls "Holy s--t!" stories to the truth.

March 3, 1989

Reporters Put Story Over Lives

Two famous TV newsmen admit getting film footage is more important than saving American soldiers' lives

When TV journalists cover wars being fought by American troops, do they go onto the battlefield as Americans who share the goals and fears of our soldiers who are risking their lives? Or do they approach their assignemnt as "objective reporters" who are completely neutral in the conflict? That question surfaced after the Grenada rescue operation in 1983, when Secretary of State George Shultz pointed out that during World War II the reporters were on our side, but that these days we could not make that assumption.

The same question surfaced during the taping of a Public Broadcasting Service program called "Under Orders, Under Fire" that is scheduled to be aired in mid-March. It is part of a PBS series titled "Ethics in America." It provides a disturbing insight into the ethics of one of America's best known television reporters, Mike Wallace, one of the stars of the CBS program, *60 Minutes*. Wallace made it clear that if he were covering a battle involving American troops he would be there strictly as a disinterested observer who would willingly trade the torn flesh and spilled blood of American soldiers for a few minutes of dramatic film footage.

The program's moderator, Charles Ogletree, Jr., a Harvard law professor, asked Peter Jennings, the anchorman on ABC's *World News Tonight* this hypothetical question. Supposed you are a TV correspondent traveling with an enemy unit that surprises American soldiers, what would you do? Peter Jennings, who is a Canadian citizen, replied, "I think I would do what I could to warn the Americans." Ogletree said, "Even if it meant not getting the live coverage?" Jennings responded in the affirmative, adding that he was glad this was only a hypothetical question.

Mike Wallace, who was playing the role of Jennings' boss back in New York, took a different position. He said, "Some reporters would have a different reaction. They would regard it simply as another story that they are there to cover." Ogletree asked, "They are going to cover enemy soldiers shooting and killing American soldiers?" Wallace said yes, and went on to express his astonishment at Peter Jennings' reaction. He said, "I'm a little bit at a loss to understand why, because you are an American, you would not have covered that story."

Professor Ogletree asked Wallace if he didn't have a higher duty as an American citizen to do all that he could to save the lives of the American soldiers rather than treating it as just another story to be covered. Mike Wallace replied, "No, you do not have a higher duty. No, no, no." Wallace's emphatic rejection of the notion that a journalist owed any higher duty to his fellow Americans caused Peter Jennings to have second thoughts. He said he thought Wallace was right and his first reply was wrong. Marine Colonel George M. Connell expressed his "utter contempt" for both Wallace and Jennings. He posed his own hypothetical situation: Wallace and Jennings were ambushed and wounded. Should he risk the lives of his troops and order them to rescue the journalists? He asked, "Would it be fair to say, 'they're just journalists,' they're not Americans? You can't have it both ways." The colonel said he would rescue them anyway. Marines would die to save a couple of journalists who wouldn't lift a finger to save a Marine.

February 21, 1989

Media Still Biased Against Pro-Lifers

TV networks prove they are incapable of covering abortion in an even-handed way

Over the years the media have been notorious in their coverage of the Surpeme Court's abortion decision. ABC's *Nightline*, one of the most respected shows on television, has had to correct itself twice after incorrectly reporting that the decision only legalized abortion during the first three months of pregnancy.

Inaccuracies aside, there is also the issue of bias. On the eve of the recent March for Life against abortion, a new study was released which found that reporters have unfairly colored the national debate on abortion through the use of biased labels. The Media Research Center charged that the national networks have proven themselves incapable of covering abortion in an even-handed way. NBC News was singled out for criticism as being less objective than the others. But typically, NBC News Washington bureau chief Robert McFarland rejected the criticism, claiming that his network goes out of its way to be fair and that NBC News believes that each side should be treated in the same way.

But that's not the way it is on network news. And the new findings came as no surprise to Nellie Gray, organizer of the March for Life. She told us, "The reason we have abortion continuing is an unprofessional press. The press reports starvation in Bangladesh and Ethiopia. But the press doesn't report the fact that 4,000 children a day are being killed through abortion." She said if 4,000 dogs were being killed daily, the cameras would be all over the carcasses.

The study examined all stories discussing abortion during the last four months of 1988 that aired on ABC's *World News*

Tonight, the CBS *Evening News*, CNN *Prime News* and NBC *Nightly News*. The analysts operated on the assumption that objective reporting requires that journalists adhere to balance in their use of labels. They said that pro-life should be used in conjunction with pro-choice, or else anti-abortion with pro-abortion. Another balanced alternative would be to offer an equal number of positive and negative labels on each side.

However, they found that when it comes to stories on abortions, the networks ignored all standards of objectivity. In the 49 stories employing labels, the anti-abortion tag was used 87 times, with another five references to abortion foes. The terms pro-life or right-to-life were used only 24 times. By contrast, the term pro-abortion was used only once. The networks preferred the pro-choice label 19 times. Thirteen other times, they were labeled by such terms as family planning advocates.

Their conclusion was that the pro-choice forces were designated by their preferred labels 97 percent of the time, while the pro-life forces were afforded their desired label only 21 percent of the time. And NBC News was the worst offender. It used the anti-abortion label 17 times, while using the pro-life label only once. NBC reporters called the other side pro-choice but never called it pro-abortion. Rather than dismiss these findings, as Robert McFarland did, NBC News President Michael Gartner should act on them.

February 2, 1989

How
Mike Wallace
Slants The News

His one-sided reporting and censorship on "60 Minutes"
completely distorted report on Honduras

Last month Mike Wallace did a report on *60 Minutes* about U. S. aid to Honduras, the Central American country bordering Nicaragua on the north where the Nicaraguan freedom fighters have had bases for several years. The thrust of Wallace's report was that the $165 million a year in economic and military aid that we have given Honduras over the past eight years has been wasted. Wallace relied heavily on the views of a far-left American named Joe Eldridge, who is an admirer of the Sandinistas and Castro and a bitter critic of our policy of supporting freedom-loving Nicaraguans who are fighting for democracy and human rights in their country.

Wallace's report was carefully crafted to make it appear that just about everyone in Honduras supported Eldridge's view that our aid has been wasted, that the Hondurans are worse off now than they were eight years ago, and that they want to see the freedom fighters forced out of Honduras and the American presence there reduced. If he interviewed the American ambassador or anyone from the American embassy, he didn't use what they said in his report. He interviewed only one Honduran government official, but only to get him to say that the economy had suffered in the past eight years, cutting off his explanation that this was because of the problems created for all Central America by Nicaragua.

But Wallace wanted to get both sides. He interviewed Elliott Abrams, the assistant secretary of state for Inter-American Affairs, a strong proponent of Reagan's policy of supporting the Nicaraguan freedom fighters. Abrams had a strong and important message that he hoped *60 Minutes* would transmit to the American people. He was disappointed. Wallace included in his report only a tiny portion of the Abrams interview, a portion in which Wallace argued that democracy in a poor country like Honduras should mean jobs, better health care and schools.

Abrams insisted that freedom, human rights and elections were important to poor countries, an idea that Mike Wallace professed not to understand. But he understood very well the important message that Abrams gave him, a message that he refused to include in his report because it clashed with the views of the left-wingers like Joe Eldridge that he was out to promote.

What Abrams told Wallace was that our aid to the Nicaraguan freedom fighters was producing the results we wanted when Congress last February undertook the experiment of denying them further military aid. He said this was done in the hope that our restraint would result in less Soviet aid to the Sandinistas, less repression in Nicaragua, less support for the communist rebels trying to overthrow the government of El Salvador and greater progress toward a peaceful solution in Central America.

Abrams said this hadn't worked, that there is more repression, more subversion and no appreciable decrease in Soviet aid. He said that the Sandinistas are no longer even talking with the Democratic Resistance, because by cutting off aid, Congress removed their incentive to do so. He warned that we would have to return to putting pressure on the Sandinistas if we didn't want to see the rest of Central America destabilized. Wallace reported none of that. He ended with a message from Joe Eldridge, that we should be nice to the Sandinistas and they would be nice to us.

February 1, 1989

53

Havana's Man In CBS

Misreporting on Cuba by Mike Wallace and Harry Reasoner on "60 Minutes"

CBS once again demonstrated its willingness to polish Fidel Castro's image in a *60 Minutes* segment aired on New Year's Day titled *Cuba: Thirty Years After.* The CBS crew didn't get an interview with Castro or even any lesser Cuban government officials. They had to settle for a radio and TV commentator named Alberto Perez, but despite the snub, Harry Reasoner obligingly transmitted the pro-Castro propaganda Perez dished out in near perfect English.

Mike Wallace started the ball rolling with the introductory observation that what Reasoner found after 30 years of Castro's rule was "a changed Cuba, some say for the better." On came Perez to tell the vast CBS audience, "There's a sense of pride, of dignity, and that's worth much more than any material goods in the world." He explained away the flight of more than a million Cubans from the island paradise, saying they were people who wanted nice cars, color TV, the opportunity to make lots of money. He said they weren't willing to make the sacrifices "necessary to provide a lot of free stuff here for people."

Reasoner didn't think to ask what was wrong with people wanting to make a good living and enjoy the consumer goods that are so abundant today in countries that were poorer than Cuba 30 years ago. When Perez assured him that Cubans today have a much better life than they had before, Reasoner said, "And as far as we could see Alberto Perez was right." When Perez assured him that there had not been "an instance of brutality, of torture, here," Reasoner showed no sign of ever having heard of Armando Valladares, the Cuban poet,

54

whose book, *Against All Hope*, recounts in detail the torture he and other victims of Castro suffered in Cuban prisons.

Perez, responding to claims that there are numerous human rights violations in Cuba, trotted out the routine communist answer that the really important human rights are "the right to eat, the right to work, the right to get medical attention, the right to education." Reasoner seemed to agree, saying, "That may be true," while acknowledging that there were problems of productivity and shortages in Cuba.

That was a fleeting concession to the harsh reality of life in Cuba today, where the meat ration is 10 ounces and the coffee ration 4 ounces a month. Reasoner gave no information on rationing. Instead, he rhapsodized about Cuban health care and education, ignoring a leaked secret study that showed a very high level of dissatisfaction with the quality of health care. Nor did he note that higher education is denied those whose thinking differs from that of the Communist Party.

In contrast, *The New York Times* ran an editorial saying, "Cuba after 30 years remains poor, unfree and dependent. And a country whose economy in 1958 was among Latin America's most advanced has skidded to the middle ranks. No wonder this tropical dictator-for-life fears a real popular judgment." Why the difference? Reasoner answered that when he revealed that *60 Minutes* had employed Saul Landau as a paid consultant. Landau is a Marxist and a notorious apologist for Castro and his revolution.

CBS got exactly what it paid for—a big dose of dishonest pro-Castro propaganda.

January 18, 1989

How CBS Helps Our Enemies

More evidence of the media's anti-American slant in reporting on Honduras

After starting off the New Year with a *60 Minutes* segment on the glorious achievements of Dictator-for-Life Fidel Castro, CBS News followed up a week later with another *60 Minutes* segment telling how bad things are in Honduras, a Central American country that is free, democratic and friendly to the United States. Unlike Cuba, where CBS correspondent Harry Reasoner acknowledged that people were afraid to criticize the regime on camera, Honduras posed no such problem for correspondent Mike Wallace. He interviewed at length two prominent Hondurans and two Americans living there, all of whom were very critical of both the Honduran government and the United States.

The Honduran program opened with an attack on the U. S. Embassy Annex in Tegucigalpa by some 300 students. Wallace described this as "an act of rage, of defiance, mainly by a few hundred students of the left and the right" to protest the forcible extradition of a Honduran drug lord to the United States. There was no indication that Wallace had interviewed anyone who participated in this attack, and he didn't make it known how he had learned that they were students from both the right and the left who were motivated by rage. The State Department claims that the agitators who stirred up the students were hired by the drug lord.

Wallace readily bought the explanation provided by one of the radical Americans he interviewed, who described it as a spontaneous "explosion" which didn't "express a particular political position," just anti-Americanism. That fitted the message that Wallace wanted to convey perfectly. He devoted nearly a minute to footage of about 25 people carrying three or four banners and placards protesting the American presence in Honduras. Wallace said the demonstrators numbered "a few hundred," and their tiny procession was shown from seven different angles to give it the appearance of greater size. The exaggeration was essential to support Wallace's description: "just another note in the wave of mounting dissatisfaction here."

Castro, of course, doesn't permit even feeble visible expressions of dissent and so CBS treated its viewers to footage of the allegedly beloved dictator addressing half a million people. Harry Reasoner didn't mention that these huge crowds are assembled because attendance is compulsory and is enforced at the workplace or school. The message in this report was that Cubans are proud and contented because things are better than they were 30 years ago (which is false), while in free Honduras people are angry and discontented because things are (arguably) worse than they were eight years ago.

The report on Honduras briefly showed three stores, all loaded with such things as Sony TV sets, Reebok shoes and fine scotch whiskey. Mike Wallace quickly dismissed such evidence of the ability of consumers to satisfy their needs. Wallace explained that U. S. aid, which has averaged $162 million a year for the past eight years, "helped support an artificially high standard of living for the very small middle and upper class." The implication was that only the rich can enjoy color television sets and other modern consumer goods, such as the nice cars that jam the streets of Honduran cities.

In the program on Cuba, the Cuban official spokesman had explained the flight of a million Cubans as being the result of their desire to enjoy nice cars and color TV. It is estimated that Cuba has received an average of $3.5 billion a year in aid from the Soviets during the past eight years, but there even such consumer goods as meat, rice, coffee, and clothing, not to mention color TVs, are in short supply. CBS didn't mention that if we were giving as much aid to Honduras per capita as the Soviets are giving Cuba, our annual aid would have totaled $1.4 billion a year, not $162 million.

57

In doing their Cuba report, *60 Minutes* used as a paid consultant Saul Landau, an American radical Marxist who admires Castro. In Honduras they leaned heavily on another American radical, Joseph Eldridge, who is also a great admirer of Castro and the Nicaraguan communists who call themselves Sandinistas. They did not describe Eldridge as a paid consultant, but he appeared frequently in the program and was clearly Wallace's guiding light. Wallace even bought the communist line that the important human rights in countries like Honduras are jobs, medical care and education, not freedom and democracy.

January 13, 1989

Misinformation
On
South Africa

The New York Times ignores the facts to give completely false view of life in South Africa

The New York Times showed itself to be completely out of touch with reality in a December 15th editorial that claimed that racial repression in South Africa may be worse today than it was in 1981. The Times claimed that South Africa has shown no inclination to negotiate an end to hostilities with its own black majority population. The South African regime, the Times said, has failed to implement internal reforms, and has failed to promote political rights for the black majority. The Times says, "after seven years, South African moderates of all races are weaker than ever."

But J. S. Kane-Berman of the South African Institute of Race Relations tells a far different story. In a recent article for *The Los Angeles Times*, this expert laid out the facts about progress in South Africa, saying, "A silent socio-economic revolution is transforming South African society, unnoticed by most foreign observers, the local and international media and many of our own political leaders." The column said that ordinary South Africans, black and white, are helping to change things for the better. By the year 2000, four out of every five school graduates will be black. By the end of the century, the South African economy will probably be the most racially integrated on earth.

Since 1979, South African workers have had official recognition from the government. Two years ago, the pass laws that prevented blacks from entering cities without permits were repealed. A law is still on the books known as the Group Areas Act, which bars blacks from living in areas designated as white, but this law is being ignored by more than 150,000

59

black people who have moved into white areas. The government is still trying to enforce the Group Areas Act, but the author says these efforts are destined to fail.

The government still restricts some black opportunities in education, but the author says universities and technical schools are now free to admit people of any race. Private schools today in South Africa are racially mixed and even subsidized. Government schools are bound to go along with these changes.

Speaking from personal experience, the author says, "What we are witnessing all around us is that one apartheid law after another is being taken apart, or rendered unworkable, by the actions of ordinary people." The only question left is how quickly political changes will follow. If they do, South Africa will have achieved racial harmony more successful than the United States has.

The New York Times ignored all of these points in its own editorial on South Africa. It said nothing about black trade union rights, the integration of society, and the elimination of the pass laws. The South African Government still deserves criticism, but the Times should not claim that no progress has been made. The Times' motto is "All the News that's Fit to Print." But on South Africa, its news judgement is that the good news should not be printed. This misinformation leads to wrong-headed policies in Washington, such as economic sanctions, which hurt the people that the Times says it wants to help.

January 5, 1989

CBS News Swallows Castro Propaganda

Misleading reporting on Cuba by Kathleen Sullivan and Bruce Morton.

On January 1, Fidel Castro will celebrate the 30th anniversary of his seizure of power in Cuba. The oppressed people of Cuba have no cause to celebrate along with their communist caudillo and his corrupt cronies, who are lagging far behind the Soviets in admitting their failures and permitting greater freedom and openness. Sad to say, while some of our Big Media journalists are now reporting the flaws, failures and fictitious claims that are being exposed in the Soviet Union under glasnost, some of them are still buying and peddling the mendacious propaganda fed to them by Fidel Castro.

CBS News sent two of its stars, Bruce Morton and Kathleen Sullivan to Cuba to cover the Gorbachev visit that didn't take place because of the Armenian earthquake. Unable to cover Gorbachev, they used the opportunity to report to viewers of the CBS *Evening News* and the *Morning Show*, which Kathleen Sullivan co-hosts, on conditions in Cuba. Broadcasting from Havana on December 8, Morton told his viewers, "Today, he (Castro) seems very popular, very much in charge. That's in spite of problems with housing, in spite of shortages. You see a lot of people standing in line in Cuban shops. On the other hand, no one goes hungry." Castro biographer and buddy, Tad Szulc, was then shown saying there is "a total absence of visible dissent" in Cuba. Morton claimed it was hard to know what Cubans really think, saying "The outspoken anti-Castro ones have left."

Indeed they have, by the hundreds of thousands. CBS could find plenty of outspoken Cubans in Miami and scores of

61

other cities in the United States, including New York. They would be more than happy to explain to Bruce Morton how the average Cuban feels about the regime that has made the same kind of mess in Cuba that the communists made in the Soviet Union and China and everywhere else they have held power.

Jose Luis Llovio-Menendez, a former senior official in the Castro regime, contrasts the lives of the Castro elite and the ordinary Cubans in his book, *Insider*. After the hardships and frustrations faced daily by "Liborio," the average Cuban, he says, "For the present, Liborio pretends, endures, waits. But his soul is filled with resentment toward those who, in the name of equality, live so well while he lives so badly. This bitterness is growing, and one day, when he finally loses his patience, the docile Liborio will sharpen his machete once again and take the offensive. . . in an explosion of uncontrollable rage."

Kathleen Sullivan displayed even greater gullibility and naivete than Morton. On the CBS *Morning Show* on December 9, she gushed about how Castro had promised to deliver quality health care to every citizen free, and how well he had delivered on that promise. She showed an impressive high-rise hospital, saying that Cuba has "hi-tech medicine." She explained that those who need specialized care can get everything from nuclear medicine to multiple organ transplants and that the care is so good that Cuba is now offering packaged surgery tours to other Latin Americans. But the real secret of Cuba's health care success, she said, were the little neighborhood clinics that emphasize preventive medicine.

It sounds wonderful, but its total falsity was exposed by a secret report prepared by the Cuban Communist Party which was smuggled out of the country and turned over to Armando Valladares. *The Washington Times* ran a story on it in September. It reported the findings of a survey of 10,756 Cubans in the province of Holguin in the latter half of 1987. This survey found that 87.6 percent of those questioned had an unfavorable opinion of the health care system, an increase of 3 percent over the previous year.

The people complained that at the showcase Lenin Hospital, "Pregnant women are left to die in the delivery room," that "most of the operations become infected," and that "the elderly are mistreated." A respondent said that "good attention is given only to friends and to those who have important positions." Similar complaints were voiced about those little clinics, which came under severe criticism for such things as the lack of doctors and the doctors' lack of interest in their patients. Sullivan obviously wasn't even aware of the existence of this refutation of the propaganda she was mouthing.

December 22, 1988

Asbestos
Danger
Exaggerated

Media disseminates wild estimates on number of deaths

Two years ago Congress was stampeded into passing the 1986 Asbestos Hazard Emergency Response Act (AHERA) without a single dissenting vote. This provided that all schools in the country, both public and private, would have to test for the presence of asbestos in their buildings. This led to the development of a new and costly asbestos detection and removal industry that has probably done far more harm than good. The program has been marked by scandal, but even worse is the evidence that the $150 to $200 billion it is estimated to cost is virtually a total waste of money.

It all started with the dissemination in the media of some wild estimates about the number of deaths supposedly caused by the presence of asbestos fibers in the air we breathe. Just ten years ago, a researcher at Mt. Sinai Hospital in New York, Dr. Irving Selikoff claimed that asbestos would cause 40,000 deaths a year from lung cancer and other lung ailments. The Occupational Safety and Health Administration followed a few months later with an even higher estimate. It issued a report saying that asbestos would kill 2 million Americans over the next 30 years. That comes to 67,000 a year.

Those figures were so highly exaggerated that they quickly came under attack by respected scientists. Sir Richard Doll, a noted scientist at Oxford University, said the figures were so wrong that "no arguments based even loosely on them should ever be taken seriously." The Congressional Office of Technology Assessment agreed, saying that the OSHA report could not be regarded as a serious contribution to scientific thought. Dr. Selikoff himself scaled down his estimate of deaths from asbestos quite drastically. He cut it in half, to 20,000 a year in 1980, and subsequently he put the number at 8,300 a year.

That is still a wild exaggeration. More recent studies have found no evidence that white asbestos, the type that is mined in Canada, poses any significant health hazard to the general public. Selikoff's estimates had been based on a study of shipyard workers who had worked with amosite, a red asbestos imported from South Africa during World War II. The study was flawed for a number of reasons, but the hysteria about asbestos was fueled by the failure to make it clear to the public that not all asbestos is alike.

A Royal Commission that studied the problem of asbestos in schools in Canada concluded that the health risk to the students was not great enough to justify the cost of removal. (It noted that removal programs might increase the risk to the workers doing the job.) A British health commission reached a similar conclusion after three years of study. Michael J. Bennett, author of a forthcoming book, *Asbestos Hysteria*, says EPA estimates that a successful ban on all asbestos might save 126 lives a year, a number that could be more than offset by deaths caused by our being forced to use less effective substitutes for fire protection and in brake linings.

The hysteria about asbestos is costing us a great deal of money, and we ought to be asking why we have been so badly misinformed. Here's a clue to the answer. *The Boston Globe* described Dr. Selikoff as "accessible to the press, always good for a snappy quote, and he offers higher estimates of risk for most asbestos related diseases than any other investigators." He gave the reporters what they wanted: bad news in an attractive package.

December 20, 1988

Pentagon
Gets Burned
By ABC

ABC program "Burning Questions" misleads

On December 1st, ABC aired a program called, *Burning Questions: The Business of Defense*. It was essentially a series of reports on waste, fraud and abuse in military spending. At the end, standing in front of a huge American flag, correspondent Tom Jarriel charged that ABC had not gotten any cooperation from the Pentagon in doing the program. Jarriel said, "What kind of statement does that make about accountability?"

But it was ABC that didn't tell the whole truth. The Pentagon did cooperate in answering questions from ABC researchers and providing background about weapons system. But it refused on-camera interviews and didn't give the network certain film of personnel and equipment. It didn't cooperate on this matter because the reporter of the ABC program, Charlie Thompson, had a bad reputation. He was responsible for several stories on the *20/20* program that Pentagon officials believed were horribly flawed. In a statement, the Pentagon said, "ABC producers explained to us last August how they planned to string together a series of 'horror stories' about faulty military equipment. They showed little or no interest in our repeated efforts 'to tell the whole story' in a balanced way that would show ABC viewers the complete cycle of the procurement process."

The Pentagon added, ". . . the subjects selected by ABC have been vigorously reported by the media. Many of the issues have been fully resolved. Re-telling old stories in a sensationalized way can confuse viewers into thinking that specific problems have not been resolved. Simply put, we were and continue to be concerned about the lack of balance of this documentary.''

What bothered Pentagon officials was the tendency of ABC to portray them in the worst possible light, and to ignore the good faith efforts that have been made to correct errors. Jarriel showed the DIVAD anti-aircraft gun, calling it a one and a half billion dollar fiasco. What he didn't point out was that it was canceled three years earlier by the Pentagon itself. Tom Jarriel reminded viewers of the $16,000 refrigerators on Navy planes as a newspaper story about this was flashed on the screen. If you could have read the story, you would have discovered that Navy officials were the ones who disclosed this example of abuse.

ABC contended that the Bradley fighting vehicle was seriously flawed. They showed film of the Bradley being hit and destroyed in training films. What they didn't mention was that these tests were designed to determine how large a weapon would be needed to destroy it. The Bradley was never designed to withstand heavy artillery. Pentagon officials say tests and other training exercises have improved the vehicle and it is now being used. The same goes for the B-1 bomber, offered by ABC as an example of something that doesn't work the way it is supposed to. Defense officials say that while the B-1 has suffered set-backs, this is true of any bomber the United States has ever developed. They say the B-1 is now in service around the world.

The ABC program was heavy on sensationalism and Hollywood hype. Perhaps that explains why ABC's regular Pentagon correspondent, Bob Zelnick, had nothing to do with the show. He realizes that the story is not as simple as ABC portrayed it, and that officials in the Pentagon are not all corrupt and evil.

December 16, 1988

Bad News
Is The
Only News

How TV concentrates on bad economic news

One of the factors working in favor of George Bush's election was the economy. On November 4th, just four days before the election, it was announced that the unemployment rate had fallen to 5.2 percent, the lowest in 14 years. Bush, apparently fearful that the major media wouldn't highlight this news, emphasized it in one of his campaign speeches.

That news was covered. But it isn't usually. A new book finds that as the economy improved during the 1980s, it received progressively less attention on network television news. The book is titled, *The Vanishing Economy: Television Coverage of Economic Affairs*. It is published by the Media Institute and written by Ted Smith, an associate professor at Virginia Commonwealth University. He analyzed the network evening news programs in three one-year periods between 1982 and 1987.

He found that in the period 1982-83, there were 5300 stories about the economy. But that declined to 4600 in 1984-85, as the economy had improved, and then only 3900 in 1986-87. During the same period, coverage of economic indicators fell 64 percent. These are the key figures showing how well the economy is doing. There was an even more dramatic drop in coverage of unemployment figures. As unemployment dropped from almost 11 percent to just over 6 percent, coverage of these important indicators fell an incredible 79 percent.

Professor Smith found that bad news about the economy was frequently the only news. And the bad economic news was often attributed to the policies of the Reagan Administration. By contrast, the Administration was seldom given credit for good economic news. It was presented as if it just happened. The major media may have felt vindicated when the stock market crashed in October 1987. The market dropped a record 24 percent. What they didn't point out was that, during the preceding 5 years, the market had staged a 250 percent increase.

On the anniversary of the stock market crash, October 19, CBS *Evening News* economics correspondent Ray Brady offered a typical gloom-and-doom account. Brady said the fact that a rumor about George Bush's personal life had caused the market to drop demonstrated how fragile the economy was. He said Wall Street was plagued by "long, slow business days." He said many Wall Streeters were seeking out psychoanalysts. Herbert Freudenberger, a psychoanalyst, said his Wall Street clients were complaining that Wall Street was "like a morgue," full of depressed people, where the telephone never rings. "With the stock business so nervous," Brady said, "others businesses on Wall Street are off." He interviewed a shoeshine man, who said he used to get more business before the crash. Now, he gets less, much less.

Brady drove the point home by concluding with what he said was an old saying in the financial community. Standing by a cemetery plot, he said, "Wall Street runs from the river to the grave yard." And that about sums up Wall Street's feelings on this, the one day it would love to forget, the anniversary of October 19th, 1987."

The market recovered quickly when the rumor about Bush proved false. Brady's gloomy analysis was equally false.

November 18, 1988

69

New Study
Indicts The Press
On Nicaragua

The American Enterprise Institute shows how the press misinformed

One major problem the next president will have to deal with is Nicaragua. President Reagan and Congress supported the freedom fighters in Afghanistan, but the freedom fighters in Nicaragua have been cut-off by Congress. The sell-out of the Nicaraguan resistance has been called a "slow motion Bay of Pigs." The ruling Communist Sandinistas in Nicaragua came to power in 1979, during the Carter Administration. But the American people were led to believe that they were not Communists.

A new study by Joshua Muravchik of the American Enterprise Institute indicts the press for its coverage of the Sandinista revolution. He writes that American news organizations often portrayed the Sandinistas in ways that blurred or obscured their true identity. He analyzed network and press coverage of the Sandinistas during the two years from July 1978 until July 1980.

In June 1979, just one month before they took power, the Sandinistas announced the appointment of a five member junta that would rule Nicaragua. Because it consisted of only one admitted Sandinista, Daniel Ortega, the American press characterized it as broad-based. *The New York Times*, for example, highlighted the claim that it included "only one guerrilla leader," and that it might be expanded to include "more moderates." What the Times failed to make clear was that two other members of the junta were fellow-travelers of the Sandinista movement. This gave the Sandinistas majority control from the start.

Days before dictator Somoza fled Nicaragua, the junta

70

announced the formation of a cabinet. Only one admitted Sandinista was in it, Tomas Borge, the minister of interior, who is in charge of the security police. Muravchik writes that the media should have recognized this for what it was. He notes that Communists in Eastern Europe used coalition governments as stepping stones to dictatorships by insisting on controlling the interior ministry.

Yet *The New York Times* and *The Washington Post* reported Borge's appointment as an encouraging development. The *New York Times* said that Borge would use his power to control more radical elements of the Sandinistas. *The Washington Post* said that Borge, though a self-proclaimed Marxist, was considered a pragmatist and would keep mavericks in line. Muravchik says the reference to radicals and mavericks made no sense because the Sandinistas were a very disciplined Marxist-Leninist organization.

Muravchik speculates that reporters for the Times and Post may have been victims of an orchestrated Sandinista campaign of disinformation. He says there is no question that the Sandinistas devoted great effort to deceiving Western reporters about the true nature of their revolution. And those journalists, eager to believe the best about the young fighters against the dictator, were too easily taken in. One of those reporters, Karen De Young of the Post, once said, "most journalists now, most Western journalists at least, are very eager to seek out guerrilla groups, leftist groups, because you assume they must be the good guys." She helped contribute to what Josh Muravchik says was not a proud chapter in the history of American journalism.

November 15, 1988

Willie Horton Is Killing Dukakis

TV networks try to portray issue as racist to hurt Bush

In the first week of August a *Wall Street Journal*/NBC poll showed Michael Dukakis leading George Bush by 49 to 39 percent. Fifty-five percent of those polled said they had a favorable opinion of the Massachusetts governor, and only 26 percent had an unfavorable view. George Bush began his campaign with criticism of Dukakis on defense and foreign policy issues. I wrote a column at that time in which I said that what would hurt Dukakis more was likely to be "an obscure prison inmate in Maryland named Willie Horton."

Willie Horton is no longer obscure. The story of how this convicted murderer, sentenced to life without possibility of parole, escaped from a Massachusetts prison while on a weekend furlough and then terrorized a Maryland couple is now known to millions of Americans. Bush and Quayle have used the Horton case to convince voters that Dukakis is more concerned about prisoners' rights than victims' rights. Dukakis has accused them of misrepresenting the facts, but he simply could not shake the burden of Willie Horton.

On October 24, two weeks before election day, with Dukakis trailing Bush by 10 points or so in most polls, Willie Horton appeared as the lead story on the network evening news broadcasts. He was propelled there by charges from the Dukakis camp that Bush campaign TV ads about the Horton case had racist overtones. The Democratic vice presidential candidate, Lloyd Bentsen, started it when George Will, on *This Week With David Brinkley*, asked him, "Do you think there's an element of Republican racist appeal in the use of Willie Horton?" Bentsen replied, "When you add it up, I think there is."

The next day, Bentsen and Dukakis aides justified that charge by citing a TV ad that had shown Willie Horton's picture, thus revealing that he was black. Bentsen said there were racist overtones in the commercial. No one listening to it would have known what color Horton was had it not been for the picture. This ad was produced and distributed by an independent campaign organization called Americans for Bush. This was totally independent of the Bush campaign, as the law requires. Nevertheless, the false impression was created that this was an official Bush campaign ad. Bentsen and the Dukakis aides who were pushing the racism charge were obviously reaching. It was a measure of their desperation that they were willing to risk giving the Horton story greater exposure in the hope of getting some mileage out of the charge of racism. They knew that Willie Horton was killing Dukakis, and they had to fight back.

It was a high risk maneuver, but they got quite a bit of help from their friends in CBS and NBC News. Dan Rather and his CBS team were very cooperative. They showed Dukakis and other Democrats denouncing the GOP's racist tactics, but they refrained from showing the Horton commercial that Bentsen had alluded to. That was helpful to Dukakis, since it avoided showing the ad to a wider audience and denied people the opportunity to decide for themselves if the racism charge had any merit. CBS also portrayed Bush as being on the defensive, giving a lot of attention to organized heckling that he encountered in Portland, Maine.

Chris Wallace, the NBC correspondent covering Dukakis, pulled a dirty trick of his own to help Dukakis. After airing the Dukakis campaign's charges of racism in the Horton commercial, Wallace said, "In addition to the Horton case, they cite a Bush ad on prison furloughs which they say shows black and Hispanic inmates." Viewers were shown a portion of the Bush "revolving door" ad which showed actors dressed like prisoners going through a revolving door and coming right back out again. The ad used 16 actors, only two of whom appeared to be black. To support the charge that this ad was racist, NBC used a close-up that focused on only four faces—one black, one maybe black, one white, one Hispanic.

73

You could see the backs of four other heads, two of which had light hair. NBC did not show the long line of actors, nearly all of whom appeared to be white.

Sam Donaldson was the least helpful to Dukakis, pointing out that he had pretended to have nothing to do with the racism charge while others in his campaign were spreading it. ABC also showed the Horton ad. Only Frederick Allen on CNN pointed out that this ad was not produced by the Bush campaign but by Americans for Bush.

October 25, 1988

Hollywood's War On Vietnam Veterans

How Hollywood and television have knocked Vietnam soldiers

Accuracy in Media has tried hard to dispel the myths about the Vietnam War. One myth, answered in the AIM film on television's Vietnam, is that we lost the war on the battlefield. In fact, our media misreported the enemy's critical 1968 Tet Offensive as an American military defeat when, in fact, it was a military victory. Another myth is that the American soldiers were psychotic baby killers. This is a myth perpetuated in movies and on television by such figures as Dan Rather. A documentary narrated by Rather on CBS in June 1988 suggested that American soldiers engaged in wholesale murder of innocent civilians, including babies, during the war, and that many vets today have serious mental problems.

But veterans are fighting back. One wrote an article for *The Wall Street Journal* in July blasting Hollywood and the media for their portrayal of Vietnam vets. The article prompted favorable replies from veterans around the country. William K. Lane, who served in the Green Berets in Vietnam, echoed our criticism. As one who was involved in the fighting during the Tet Offensive, he said he remembered the victory over the North Vietnamese, and he recalled "the hatred we felt when *The New York Times* clips arrived claiming the Vietnamese and American victory in the Tet Offensive was actually a defeat."

He complained that television news portrays the two typical vets as bearded, wearing fatigues, one with a pony tail. He says they are usually shown hugging and sobbing when a Vietnam memorial is unveiled. Another image is that of the American soldier as racist, neurotic and drug crazed. While there are veterans from Vietnam and other wars who have problems and who should be cared for, Lane says he has yet to meet a vet who fits the media and Hollywood stereotype.

He added, "The men I knew in Vietnam didn't hate each other because of race. We weren't on drugs. We didn't murder civilians. We didn't hate the Army or LBJ or our country. We didn't feel America owed us a free ride because we spent time defending it." He said Vietnam vets deserve better than to be caricatured by Hollywood and represented in the media as a legion of losers.

Many vets agreed and responded with letters to the Journal. The response was so dramatic that one newspaper, *The Omaha World Herald*, ran an editorial about what might be called the silent majority of Vietnam vets—those who haven't sought attention, and who have simply fit into American society. One veteran responded to William Lane's column saying, "I am tired of the whining, sniffing, paranoid image of the Vietnam vet. We're ordinary folks living ordinary lives." Another said, "In the 20 years since my Vietnam tour, I have watched with amazement at the parade of flakes projected by the media as representing Vietnam veterans."

But Vietnam vets have to do more than just write letters. They have to take action against people like Dan Rather, who have perpetuated these vicious and damaging stereotypes.

October 18, 1988

NBC
Violates
Its Own Rules

A case of irresponsible journalism on the "Today" show

The new president of NBC News, Michael Gartner, wrote a column for *The Wall Street Journal* on August 11th complaining about the use of anonymous sources. He said the "anonymous source is taking over journalism . . . It's a lousy trend that is eroding the credibility of newspapers and adding to the irresponsibility of newspapers." He could have added that it is hurting the reputation of networks, such as NBC.

About two weeks later, the NBC *Today* show aired an interview with two so-called journalists who viciously savaged George Bush's tenure as director of the CIA. They claim to have talked to hundreds of people who worked for or with Bush at the agency. But they didn't name one. It was a classic case of hiding behind the use of anonymous sources. It was irresponsible journalism that doesn't belong on Michael Gartner's network. But the so-called interview was flawed for other reasons as well. The correspondent who conducted it, Ken Bode, has a background in Democratic politics. He has a vested interest in making George Bush look bad. During the whole interview, he didn't once call on the journalists to name one of their sources. He simply accepted their claim that they had conducted over a hundred interviews with people who had worked for or with Bush at the CIA.

Bode's two journalists, Scott Armstrong and Jeff Nason, are, in fact, political operatives masquerading as journalists. Although Armstrong once worked for the *Washington Post*, he and Nason are now staffers at a group called the National Security Archive. Members of this group believe the Iran arms affair was a terrible criminal enterprise that requires jail terms for its participants and requires radical changes in the

77

foreign policy apparatus of the United States. This group supplied information to Dan Rather when he staged his ambush interview of George Bush over the Iran arms affair.

Bode not only covered up Armstrong and Nason's political colors, he failed to inform viewers about the radical make-up of the magazine in which their article on Bush appeared. Bode identified it as *Mother Jones* magazine, and said nothing more, as if it is on the same level as *U.S. News and World Report*. *Mother Jones*, in fact, is a left-wing magazine named after a self-proclaimed socialist, Mary Harris "Mother" Jones. One question Bode should have asked of Armstrong and Nason was why they had to resort to using a magazine like *Mother Jones* as an outlet for their questionable material.

Armstrong and Nason used NBC's valuable air time to accuse Bush, as CIA director, with failing to curb abuses at the agency and looking the other way when foreign intelligence services operated inside the United States. Bode concluded by saying that NBC provided the Bush office with an advance copy of the article and requested a spokesman to comment on it. But, Bode said, they declined. Well, it's no wonder that the campaign refused to respond to an article based on anonymous sources. And it's surprising that NBC became a publicity agent for a magazine called *Mother Jones*.

September 26, 1988

Media Join
Scare Campaign
Over Grapes

Tom Schell of ABC News misleads

United Farm Workers leader Cesar Chavez attracted enormous media attention with his 36-day fast designed to inspire a boycott of California table grapes. His ploy failed, but the media may have convinced many Americans that there is something to his claim that the pesticides used on grapes pose a horrible danger to human health. That is because the media generally played down or ignored the other side of the story—the lack of evidence for his claim and his political motives.

The table grape boycott was actually launched back in 1984. Massachusetts Governor Michael Dukakis and other liberals endorsed it the following year. The current campaign has received the support of more than 20 Hollywood stars. On August 18th the *Phil Donahue* show featured Ralph Nader endorsing the grape boycott. Donahue said the chemicals used on grapes had caused cancer in animals.

A report by Tom Schell of ABC News on August 21st could have been produced by Chavez's union. It showed Chavez being helped to his seat at a Catholic mass where he broke his fast by taking communion. It showed him wiping tears from the eyes of his mother as she cried about his physical state. It showed him taking a piece of bread from Ethel Kennedy, widow of Robert Kennedy, who had assisted Chavez during a previous grape boycott. Old film clips of Robert Kennedy and Cesar Chavez were also shown. Finally Chavez was shown passing on a small cross to the Reverend Jesse Jackson. Reporter Tom Schell said this symbolized "sharing the burden of the continuing fast for life." Schell said Jackson and other celebrities were going to start their own three day fasts "in the hope of stopping the use of dangerous pesticides."

That was unprofessional editorializing on the part of Tom Schell. There is no evidence that the use of pesticides on grapes is dangerous. He simply played into Chavez's hands with that statement. He was taking one of Chavez's claims and treating it as fact. Apparently, Schell didn't even bother to get the other side of the story from Bruce Obbink, president of the California Table Grape Commission. Obbink acknowledges that federal- and state-sanctioned agricultural chemicals are used in producing grapes and just about every food one can imagine. But he adds, "Year after year grapes are tested by federal and state agencies and at no time have these tests found grapes with illegal residues."

A somewhat better report on the controversy aired on the NBC *Nightly News* on August 19th. Reporter David Burrington noted the curious fact that Chavez's union membership has dropped by half in ten years and that he doesn't have a single contract with grape growers. Burrington said union officials place the blame for this on enforcement of the state farm labor law but that others say Chavez is to blame for being more interested in politics than organizing.

That law gives workers the right to elect or reject any specific union as their representatives. Most workers were at one time under a contract with Chavez's union but today no longer are. Some critics of Chavez see the scare campaign and boycott as designed to force the growers and workers into signing contracts exclusively with Chavez's union.

September 6, 1988

Boston Paper's Disinformation Exposed

Unverified charges of battlefield atrocities reported as facts

The Boston Phoenix, which boasts that it is Boston's largest weekly, ran a front page story in its April 15 edition with the headline, "The Contra Vampires, New Charges of Battlefield Atrocities." The paper claimed that it had a videotape of a "purported eyewitness" who charged that the Nicaraguan freedom fighters killed and drained the blood from peasant children to use in battlefield blood transfusions. *The Phoenix* claimed that it had "authenticated the tape." Philip Averbuck, an editor of a Massachusetts-based newsletter, *Conflict and Response*, checked into the story with some interesting results.

The charge was made by Benigna Mendiola, identified as a member of the Nicaraguan General Assembly and a foe of the Resistance. *The Phoenix* said she had seen with her own eyes the evidence that the freedom fighters had drained the blood from the bodies of four or five children for use in transfusions. But it turned out that on the videotape, Ms. Mendiola had not claimed to have actually seen the bodies herself. She had been told the story by a friend. Moreover, she didn't claim that the atrocity had taken place in May or June of 1987, as *The Boston Phoenix* had reported. It supposedly happened three years earlier, in 1984.

The author of the article, Bruce Berman, acknowledged that he was mistaken in having described Ms. Mendiola as a "purported eyewitness," but his editor, Mark Jurkowitz, nevertheless defended the article. He claimed they had followed "good, standard journalistic practices." They had done some interviews, in addition to viewing the videotape. The story carried 11 references to sources opposed to the free-

81

dom fighters, of which only two were identified. There were two citations from sources who defended the freedom fighters. The only confirmation of the charge came from an unidentified Sandinista official and an unnamed source in the U.S. Senate.

The author defended this, saying it was understandable that the sources would not want to be identified in this situation. Philip Averbuck took the trouble to check the story out with some sources that didn't mind being identified. He sent a copy of it to Maj. Roger Miranda, who was a top aide to the Nicaraguan Minister of Defense, Humberto Ortega, until last October when he defected to this country. Maj. Miranda commented: "I have absolutely never heard of such a thing. The story is obviously Soviet-type propaganda."

Mr. Averbuck also contacted the director of the Washington office of the Nicaraguan Association for Human Rights, Antonio Tejerino. This is a group that the U. S. Congress had created to monitor charges of human rights violations by both sides in Nicaragua. Mr. Tejerino said, "I have heard nothing about such denunciations. Not even the Nicaraguan government has ever made such a claim." Even the director of the Washington office of "Witness for Peace," a pro-Sandinista group, said he had never heard of this.

We found in Vietnam that our own media were very reluctant to report communist atrocities, arguing that such stories were difficult to verify. But those like *The Boston Phoenix*, who are opposed to the anti-communist freedom fighters in Nicaragua, are not at all reticent about using unverified atrocities charges to bolster their case.

August 11, 1988

82

Lesley Stahl Covers For Dukakis

She misreports on Willie Horton parole

The media have an important responsibility in this political campaign. They have to determine if there's any truth behind the political charges the candidates make against each other. George Bush has hit Michael Dukakis hard over the issue of crime, charging that Dukakis presided over the most liberal criminal furlough program in the nation. The CBS *Evening News* recently made it clear it doesn't think much of the Bush charge.

In a broadcast on July 20th, Dan Rather accused Bush of running a "classic negative campaign" by claiming Dukakis was soft on crime. Rather implied that Bush was just playing politics. The report that followed by Lesley Stahl suggested that Bush had no legitimate reason to attack Dukakis on the furlough issue.

Stahl showed Cliff Barnes and his wife Angela. Stahl accurately described them as victims of the Massachusetts furlough program. She said, "Last April Massachusetts let Willie Horton, a convicted murderer out of prison for a weekend even though he'd been sentenced to life without parole. Horton broke into Barnes' home, bound and stabbed Mr. Barnes, and raped his wife." Stahl showed Bush making two statements. They were: "What did the Democratic Governor of Massachusetts think he was doing when he let convicted first degree murderers out on weekend passes? In no other state would a cold blooded murderer like Willie Horton have been set free to terrorize innocent people."

Lesley Stahl implied that Bush was not telling the truth. She said, "But Massachusetts is hardly alone. Thirty two other states have furlough programs for convicted murderers

83

and when Ronald Reagan was governor of California, several furloughed prisoners escaped. One of them murdered a Los Angeles policeman." But Lesley Stahl was wrong. Massachusetts *was* alone. And the incident that occurred under Governor Reagan is not similar to the Willie Horton case under Governor Dukakis.

As Lesley Stahl admitted in her introduction, the Massachusetts program gave furloughs to murderers without the possibility of parole. That is what makes the program unique. *The New York Times* made the same point in a July 5th article. The Times said Massachusetts "was the only state to permit furloughs for prisoners serving a sentence of life without parole . . . ." The furlough programs in the other states were different. What Lesley Stahl didn't say about the California case was that the prisoner who escaped was not a convicted murderer. He was a burglar.

Robert James Bidinotto has written an authoritative article about the Massachusetts program in the July issue of *Reader's Digest*. He told us the following, "Massachusetts was the only state to routinely grant unescorted leave or furloughs to convicted killers sentenced to life without parole. Until its 1988 ban on furloughs for life-without-parole inmates, Massachusetts was one of the three most lenient states in dealing with murderers, as measured by a combination of, one, no death penalty for any murderers and, two, granting unescorted furloughs to lifers." Referring to media misinformation about the program, he said, "Published claims . . . that the lifer furlough program in Massachusetts is comparable to those existing in many or most other states are simply not true."

August 5, 1988

Gumbel
Is A
Bumbler

Bryant Gumbel tries to make Tawana Brawley case a racial issue

Bryant Gumbel, host of NBC's *Today* show, is one of the most prominent blacks on television. As a result, he comes under pressure from the liberal black leadership in this country to promote their causes and ideas, one of which is that racism is on the rise against blacks. On *Today* on June 23rd, Gumbel alleged that there is a pattern of injustice to blacks, and he produced two people who were supposed to prove it.

Surveying the country, Gumbel said he found alleged victims of white racism in New York, Texas, and Los Angeles. He began with a ludicrous example, that of Tawana Brawley. He described the case this way: "She's the 16 year old girl who claims that she was the victim of a racial and sexual attack in upstate New York. On the advice of her attorneys, she has refused to cooperate with law enforcement officials because, they claim, both the justice system and those that run it are racist." He also said the case was a "racially-charged puzzle."

Actually, by the time Gumbel spoke those words, the puzzle was coming together, and the Tawana Brawley case was beginning to look like an elaborate hoax designed by publicity-seeking black activists to inflame racial tensions. A good question for his guests would have been what to do about phony charges of racism in today's society.

Instead, Gumbel assumed the Brawley case was somehow legitimate and he proceeded to ask Laura Blackburne of the NAACP and Morris Dees of the Southern Poverty Law Center about the amount of racism in the criminal justice system. "It's riddled with racism," Blackburne said. Dees said there is still racism in the south. Ironically, however, the discussion seemed to indicate that racism was worse in the north than the south.

Liberal black leaders have repeatedly claimed that the Reagan Administration has fueled racism in this country. Benjamin Hooks of the NAACP says, without evidence, that racism is on the rise. Bryant Gumbel did nothing to dispel that myth, even though one of his guests, Morris Dees, said at a conference last March: "The Reagan Justice Department has done a better job enforcing the civil rights laws against racial violence than any other Administration I've dealt with in the past thirty years." Gumbel didn't bring up that quote, and neither did Morris Dees. That quote was brought to our attention by John Eastman of the U.S. Civil Rights Commission. When he asked where it had been reported, he said, "Nowhere. I was at the conference." He added that Dees got booed when he said it, because all of the other speakers and many members of the audience were completely anti-Reagan. Eastman said he has provided this quote to several members of the press, who jot it down and then ignore it.

It is a sad commentary on the media that praise for the Reagan Administration's record on civil rights from a liberal is not newsworthy. Charles McCluskey has an even worse opinion of the reporters covering the Tawana Brawley case in his home town of Wappingers Falls, New York. McCluskey, the editor of a weekly paper, calls them presstitutes. He says they have ignored the holes in the story in order to promote a racial incident. Bryant Gumbel should have him on the *Today* show.

July 14, 1988

CBS
Swallows
The Brawley Story

"CBS Evening News" with Dan Rather and Barry Petersen also tries to make case a racial issue

There have been some incredible twists and turns in the case of Tawana Brawley, the fifteen year-old black girl who initially claimed she was kidnapped and raped by six white men. A former aide to Brawley's attorneys now admits it was a hoax from the beginning.

But the CBS *Evening News* with Dan Rather treated it as legitimate in a report by Barry Petersen that aired back on February 10th. This was at a time when doubts about the case had already surfaced. Rather introduced Petersen's story this way: "The Anti-Defamation League of B'Nai B'Brith today charged that violence against blacks and Jews has escalated in the past six years. The report said that even though there are fewer hate groups, the acts of violence include bombing, armed robberies and murder. And today, Barry Petersen reports, activists pointed as an example to the specter of hate in a small community in New York State."

Rather's introduction was obviously designed to suggest that the Brawley story could very well be true, because of the escalating violence against blacks in the country at large. He did not mention that the Anti-Defamation League report is not scientific in any way. In fact, according to John Eastman of the U. S. Civil Rights Commission, nobody knows if there has been an escalation in racial violence. He tells us, "There are no nationwide statistics collected to be able to verify one way or another." He acknowledges that there is a perception of increasing racial incidents, but in his opinion that is because the press has given the matter a lot more attention since the Howard Beach incident. There was another problem with Rather's introduction. He referred to armed robberies and murders against blacks and Jews. These are certainly acts of violence, but he cited no evidence that they were racially motivated in any way.

After that inflammatory introduction, Petersen showed film of Tawana Brawley crying. Petersen said "people who have never met her think what she says happened to her represents something evil in this country." Bill Cosby was then shown calling for justice in the case. Near the end of his report, Petersen made his only reference to the doubts about the case. He said, "The facts surrounding Tawana Brawley's case remain cloudy." This was a curious way to refer to the lack of evidence that she was raped and the testimony of her neighbors disputing her account of what had happened. "But the effect is clear," Petersen said. "It is sending shock waves throughout this nation's civil rights establishment."

Benjamin Hooks of the NAACP then appeared on the air, saying, "I don't think there's any question that there's been an increase in racial violence, and most of us who have dealt with the criminal justice system have never felt it's been fair to minorities and blacks in this nation." Hooks was wrong, but Petersen didn't say so, because that would have taken the edge off his attempt to inflame racial tensions.

Finally, Petersen accepted the Brawley story as legitimate. He described it as a case "that is putting a small northern town on trial, as a test of just how much progress this nation has made in its race relations and how far it has to go." Again, Petersen was wrong. It is turning out to be a case of how gullible reporters really are.

July 12, 1988

88

Scandal
The Media
Won't Expose

Full analysis of Mighty Mouse snorting cocaine cartoon

In 1986, Lino Graglia, a brilliant law professor at the University of Texas was under consideration for a federal judgeship. He was dropped from consideration after the media stirred up a fuss over the fact that five years earlier he had reportedly used the word "pickaninny" in one of his lectures. That was advanced as evidence that he was racist and therefore unqualified to sit on the federal bench.

A few years before Prof. Graglia uttered that fateful word, Ralph Bakshi produced a feature animated cartoon called "Coonskin." It was immediately attacked by the Congress of Racial Equality as racist and was promptly withdrawn from distribution. Unlike Prof. Graglia, however, Mr. Bakshi found this was no barrier to his advancement in his profession. Today he is producing children's cartoons for CBS. No one seems to think that having once produced a racially offensive cartoon should disqualify Mr. Bakshi from making TV cartoons for the kiddies. We clearly are more concerned about the purity of mind of our judges than of artists who influence the minds of our young children.

Since I don't watch TV cartoons, I can't say whether or not Ralph Bakshi has ever tried to insinuate any racist ideas into the minds of his young viewers. But it has come to light that one of Mr. Bakshi's cartoons, an episode of *Mighty Mouse*, includes a brief scene in which the hero is seen inhaling a powdery substance up his nostrils. This was spotted by two youngsters, ages 6 and 10, in December 1987. After watching the cartoon on videotape, they told their mother that Mighty Mouse had done something bad, he had snorted cocaine. Their mother, Pam Bowen, looked at it and agreed with their interpretation.

She showed the tape to the skeptical manager of the CBS affiliate in Chico, California, Dino Corbin. He agreed that it appeared that Mighty Mouse had snorted coke, but to confirm his judgment, he showed the tape to eight of his employees. He says when he asked them what they thought the mouse was doing, they replied, "Hey, Mighty Mouse is doing a line." Mr. Corbin didn't like the idea of his station airing a cartoon showing a coke-snorting mouse, and he brought it to the attention of CBS. He was put in touch with Ralph Bakshi and Judy Price, vice president for children's programming at CBS. They told him that what he and every one else thought was cocaine was just crushed flower petals. They didn't explain why the flower petals disappeared up Mighty Mouse's nose, but Mr. Corbin was reassured when he was told that the "flower-petal-snorting" scene would be edited out before the cartoon was aired again.

But it wasn't. The cartoon, unedited, was run two more times. Last April a mother in Kansas taped the cartoon and saw Mighty Mouse inhaling the powder. She brought it to the attention of Don Wildmon, head of the American Family Association. Wildmon was also skeptical until he saw the tape. He had others watch, and they all agreed that Mighty Mouse was snorting coke. Wildmon made his complaint to CBS available to the media.

The liberal media, which are quick to make a news story out of the use of the word "pickaninny," were more inclined to poke fun at Wildmon's charge than to investigate it. Had they investigated they would have learned that Ralph Bakshi, in addition to a racially offensive cartoon, had also produced *Fritz the Cat*, a cartoon glorifying both drug use and promiscuous group sex. You might think that the production of racist and drug-glorifying pornographic cartoons should disqualify one from producing children's cartoons from television. Surely, if a producer with such a background turned out a cartoon showing the hero using drugs, the media would be quick to expose him as a menace to our young children.

If you think that, you're wrong. On July 6, AIM and the

American Family Association had a screening of the Mighty Mouse cartoon, courtesy of CBS. We invited the media, along with members of Congress, government officials and representatives of a number of organizations. Some 30 people attended, including a Congressman, some Congressional aides, and several reporters. The image on the screen was sharp. They could clearly see the powdery substance in Mighty Mouse's palm disappear up his nostrils. CBS was still contending that it was "stems, tomatoes and crushed flowers," but no one in the group found that explanation plausible. Just in case, I took along such a mixture and offered $1,000 to anyone who would inhale it up his nose. There were no takers.

How much did the public hear about this expose of Ralph Bakshi and the CBS cover-up? The UPI put out a story, which was carried by papers in Chicago and Los Angeles, but not in such major cities as Washington, New York, Philadelphia and Baltimore. CNN sent a camera crew and interviewed Rep. Benjamin Gilman, Don Wildmon and me, but the Washington bureau killed the story. The AP and major papers such as *The Washington Post*, *The Washington Times* and *The New York Times* didn't even cover the event. The word "pickaninny" may make news, but it is hard to get the media to report scandalous conduct and a cover-up by one of their own.

July 8, 1988

CBS
Smears
Vietnam Veterans

Details of Dan Rather's shocking documentary, "The Wall Within," attacking Vietnam vets

If you thought that all our major media had turned over a new leaf and were honoring our Vietnam veterans rather than portraying them as brutes, baby-killers, drug addicts and psychotics, think again. CBS and Dan Rather have renewed the attack.

On June 2, Rather narrated an hour-long documentary titled *The Wall Within*, which he described to a reporter as part of an effort to preserve "the crown jewel" of CBS News, the television documentary. He said this was "a tattered banner we are trying to keep flying." Over the years, CBS News has produced a lot of slanted, inaccurate documentaries that have contributed to the near demise of the species. Many of these have defamed and insulted our military services and our fighting men. *The Wall Within* fits into that dishonorable tradition.

Superficially, the program dripped with sympathy for Vietnam veterans. It dealt with the psychological suffering experienced by some who fought in that war and who claim to bear deep emotional scars as a result of the horrible things they did and saw in Vietnam. Dan Rather informed us, inaccurately, that about a third of the Vietnam veterans are now suffering from PTSD (post-traumatic stress disorder). He said, inaccurately, that between 26,000 and 100,000 had committed suicide.

Rather proceeded to interview half a dozen men who claimed to be suffering from Vietnam-induced PTSD. "Claimed" is the proper word, because Rather does not indicate that any effort was made to corroborate the stories he was told by these emotionally disturbed men from military records or from Veterans Administration medical records. One man, who didn't want to give his full name on the air, claimed that he had been part of the Phoenix program in Vietnam and had engaged in such activities as wiping out Vietnamese villages, murdering the inhabitants and then putting the blame on the Viet Cong. He claimed this was done for propaganda purposes. He said that after coming home he became a victim of drug and alcohol abuse and had tried to kill his own mother. All of this he attributed to the trauma of his experiences as an "assassin" in Vietnam.

The man claimed to have been a Navy Seal, but William Colby, the former director of Central Intelligence who headed the Phoenix program in Vietnam, says that there were no Navy Seals in the operation. He said that at his confirmation hearing in 1971, the more sensational charges that were made about the Phoenix program were all by people who had nothing to do with it. That description obviously fits the man Rather interviewed. If the fellow tried to kill his mother, it isn't surprising that he might have tried to blame it on the trauma of the Vietnam War. He wouldn't be the first to try to use that as an excuse for criminal conduct. CBS obviously didn't verify the story itself, and by concealing the name of the accuser, it makes it difficult for anyone else to do so.

Another of Rather's interviewers was a seriously disturbed man named Terry Bradley. He claimed to have been ruined by "the awful stuff inside" him. Asked to describe it, he said, "Let's say could you go up to 50 people in an hour . . . and go out and get a knife and skin 'em? Get babies' arms, eyeballs, guts and hold their heart in your hand and throw them in piles? Could you do this for one hour of your life, just stack up every way a body could be mangled, up into body, an arm, a tit, an eyeball . . . and stuff like this and them pile them up? You do this just an hour, let's say, and not have this inside you all your life? Okay, imagine us over there for a year doing this continuously . . . ."

These were the ravings of a psychotic, and Rather knew it. He hasn't demanded an investigation and court-martial of those responsible for these alleged atrocities. By airing the charges, he has smeared both our veterans and our country.

Rather greatly exaggerated the number of veterans who have committed suicide and who suffer PTSD. Their suicide rate is about the same as the general population's. A recent study by the Center for Disease Control showed that only 15 percent of the Vietnam veterans had ever suffered combat-related PTSD, and only 2 percent experienced the disorder in the month prior to the examination. Unlike CBS, the CDC study found that the overwhelming majority of Vietnam vets are normal, well-adjusted people. They weren't baby-killers in Vietnam, and they are not mother-murderers in civilian life.

June 3, 1988

Media
Fire Guns
At Bush

New York Times and Washington Post try to "get" Bush on Noriega and drugs

George Bush has already clinched the 1988 Republican presidential nomination, and one issue that the Democrats and the media are going to use against him is drugs. The main charge has been that Bush, as vice president and earlier as CIA director, dealt with Panama General Manuel Noriega at a time it was known he was a drug smuggler. On May 8th, the big guns of the liberal media, *The Washington Post* and *New York Times*, hit Bush hard on this issue. Both papers missed their target.

The Post published a front page story about charges that Bush has not told the truth about what he knows on this matter. Bush was reported as saying that he learned of Noriega's drug involvement when the general was indicted in Florida three months ago. The Post admitted, "The available record contains no information establishing that Bush knew of the information about Noriega's link to drugs." So much for the Post's big front page story.

On that very same day, *The New York Times* weighed in with its artillery against Bush. In its front page story, the Times claimed that Bush had been told nearly three years ago by the American Ambassador to Panama that Noriega was involved in drugs. The Times' sources were said to be Administration officials. A spokesman for Bush was quoted as saying that the Vice President did not recall the subject of Noriega and drugs coming up at that meeting. Inside the story the Times acknowledged, "The Noriega issue could play a role in the fall election campaign." That is undoubtedly why

95

both the Times and the Post have decided to give the issue so much play.

But the Times story also backfired. The former Ambassador to Panama, Edward Everett Briggs, who is now Ambassador to Honduras, held a news conference to dispute *The New York Times*. He stated categorically, "I could not have briefed the Vice President on Noriega's drug running, drug smuggling or money laundering activities because we simply did not have evidence of those activities at that time, and so any statement to the effect that I did brief him on such matters at that time simply is not true."

In contrast to the front page coverage given the anonymous Administration officials, Briggs' categorical on-the-record denial was covered by the Times in a small story at the bottom on page 17. Incredibly, the Times added an editor's note to the story questioning whether Briggs' comments were meant to directly dispute the Times story. That should have been obvious.

The Times story broke on Sunday, just in time for it to become a topic on that day's interview programs. Sure enough, it was raised on the NBC program *Meet the Press*. The issue suddenly changed from whether Bush knew about Noriega's drug ties to Senator Chris Dodd's point that he should have known. Asked for comment, a spokesman for Bush responded that the Democrats could continue to try to make it an issue because "They don't have anything else to talk about." But that's not really true, either. The Democrats could be asked to explain why the Carter Administration played down reports on Panama's role in drug smuggling when Jimmy Carter was trying to get the Panama Canal Treaty passed by the Senate. Our media have shown no interest in getting to the bottom of that.

May 18, 1988

Another Smear Job From PBS

PBS tries to pin drug trafficking in Laos and Vietnam on CIA

The CIA has been taking a beating from PBS, the Public Broadcasting Service. In April, PBS aired a film featuring charges that the CIA tried to kill former Nicaraguan resistance leader Eden Pastora in 1984. Tomorrow, PBS is scheduled to air a program called, *Guns, Drugs and the CIA*. A press release for the show says that it will investigate "the forty year history of the CIA's involvement with drug lords around the world."

One part of the program is supposed to focus on what was called the secret war in Laos during the Vietnam conflict. The PBS press release claims, "To fight the clandestine war in Laos, the CIA enlisted Hmong tribesmen, trained them, equipped them, and turned them into a secret army. And according to former CIA agents, pilots and other American officials who participated in the war in Laos, the CIA's hand picked Hmong leader, Vang Pao, used CIA money and its airline, Air America, to further increase his share of the Southeast Asian heroin trade—heroin that often ended up in the veins of American soldiers in Vietnam."

Based on the press release, the producers interviewed only one person who refuted these allegations. That was Air Force Major General Richard Secord, who served in the secret war in Laos. Secord denies that Americans assisted Vang Pao in any widespread drug trafficking.

The program apparently ignores the fact that the Senate Intelligence Committee thoroughly investigated CIA operations and Air America during the time in question. It concluded, "On the basis of its examination, the Committee has con-

97

cluded that the CIA air proprietaries did not participate in illicit drug trafficking."

The denials come from many different individuals who had some involvement in that conflict. Former CIA director William Colby said the agency took all possible steps against drug trafficking, particularly in Laos, where opium had been a major product. Colby says, "When we set up our programs to help the people fight off the North Vietnamese, we took steps to try to get them on to other crops. We prohibited the transport of that stuff on our aircraft, Air America." Ted Shackley says that during the time he served as CIA station chief in Laos, the agency spot checked for drugs being smuggled on Air America flights.

Former deputy director of the CIA, George Carver, says there may be a small kernel of truth behind the PBS program. Since opium was a major crop in the region, he says it is possible that some of the Hmong or some Americans could have stashed a few poppyseeds in a napsack aboard an Air America flight. But he points out this does not constitute a major drug smuggling operation, and it does not indicate that the CIA approved of it in any way. Carver was upset when he learned that the program would portray Vang Pao as a major drug smuggler. Carver said Vang Pao deserves praise for his efforts in keeping two North Vietnamese divisions at bay throughout the war. That was a role he said that the North Vietnamese never forgave him for.

May 16, 1988

Media Still Gentle On Jesse Jackson

How John Chancellor misled on Jackson's past

Jesse Jackson's hopes of winning the Democratic presidential nomination are fading fast, but he obviously expects to exert a strong influence in shaping the Democratic Party platform. He is very unlikely to get the vice presidential nomination, but if Dukakis is elected Jackson and his supporters will be keenly disappointed if he is not given an influential post in the new administration.

For this reason, Jackson's character and views are still a matter of public concern, but most of the news media are still helping Jackson cover up the skeletons in his closet. Not many journalists have been as blatantly protective of Jackson as NBC's veteran commentator, John Chancellor. On the NBC *Nightly News* on April 6, Chancellor discussed the complaint that "if the press would only do its job and investigate Jackson, it would find damaging facts."

Chancellor said *The Chicago Tribune* had been investigating Jackson for some 15 years and had given him "a real scrubbing" a few years ago. Chancellor said, "In terms of his own finances and his economic lifestyle, the Tribune's investigators came up with no evidence of wrongdoing."

Chancellor then said, "There are old allegations about Jackson's relations with women. He and his wife answered questions on that subject when he became a candidate last year. Last fall, *The Atlanta Journal and Constitution* took a long, extremely detailed look at his personal life and found no new evidence of any misbehavior."

Finally, the NBC commentator found one minor flaw in Jackson's record that the press had uncovered. It was the report by the *Champaign* (Ill.) *News-Gazette* that Jackson was

99

not truthful in saying that "he left the University of Illinois in 1960 because the school would not allow a black to be quarterback on the football team." Chancellor allowed that was not the case, since the paper had found that "the man who did play quarterback for Illinois that year was, in fact, black."

Chancellor concluded: "That's about it as far as investigative stories are concerned. The press hasn't buried scandals about Jackson because he's black. As far as we know, there are no scandals to report."

John Chancellor's survey of Jackson's skeletons barely scratched the surface, but in addition, he was glaringly misleading in his treatment of the three cases he discussed. *The Chicago Tribune* and others have reported that federal audits of Jackson's Operation PUSH-EXCEL found that 28 percent of the $4.9 million in federal grants to this organization had been spent improperly or could not be accounted for. The government has been trying for years to get the $1.4 million that was misspent or unaccounted for returned.

Jackson has been accused by his biographer, Barbara Reynolds, who is black, of having a record of marital infidelity that would rival Gary Hart's. Far from answering questions about this, both Jackson and his wife have labeled questions about this Baptist minister's alleged adultery as "vulgar" and "inappropriate." *The Atlanta Journal and Constitution*, whose investigation was cited by Chancellor as justifying his dismissal of the allegations, actually said that reports of affairs have dogged Jackson all his married life and that in the past four years "he's been tied to two prominent women in Washington-based black organizations, as well as a woman now involved in his campaign."

Finally, Chancellor, in acknowledging that Jackson had lied about the reason he left the University of Illinois, failed to state what the *Champaign News-Gazette* reported to be the real reason. That was that he had been caught in an act of plagiarism, the same misdeed that brought Senator Joe Biden's campaign to a grinding halt.

There are many other skeletons in Jesse Jackson's closet. These include his having falsely claimed to having cradled the mortally-wounded Martin Luther King, Jr. in his arms, the presence on his staff of Jack O'Dell, a man who was identified in sworn testimony as a member of the Communist Party, and charges that his Operation PUSH was used to enrich his half-brother and his cronies. NBC News insists that Mr. Chancellor was not "misreporting" when he said there were no scandals to report even as it admits that these many scandals have been reported by some media. That is another scandal.

May 6, 1988

Cagney
And Lacey
Propaganda
How entertainment programs are used to influence public

Parade magazine recently ran a puff-piece about Dorothy Swanson and her group Viewers for Quality Television, but it's doubtful that Dorothy Swanson knows quality when she sees it. The article credits her with saving the CBS program *Cagney and Lacey* from cancellation. *Cagney and Lacey* has proven itself to be liberal propaganda masquerading as entertainment.

In 1985, for example, the National Right to Life Committee denounced an episode of the program as "a piece of pure political propaganda." The episode featured both of the characters, Cagney and Lacey, coming down on the pro-abortion side of the argument. It portrayed opponents of abortion as fanatics who bomb clinics. The executive producer actually screened the episode for pro-abortion groups prior to its showing on national television. One of the characters later defended the program in a speech to the National Abortion Rights Action League.

In 1986, *Cagney and Lacey* took the far left view of events in South Africa. The program made the ridiculous claim that South Africa's treatment of blacks is like Nazi Germany's treatment of Jews. It ridiculed the evidence that Communists are either behind or taking advantage of the unrest in that country. Another message was that those opposed to business disinvestment in South Africa are only interested in protecting their profits, and that South Africa's strategic materials are of no importance to the United States.

The California table grape industry took exception to a 1987 *Cagney and Lacey* program which incorporated dialogue that grapes were hazardous and that various characters would not have become ill if they had either not eaten grapes or if they had supported a grape boycott. The program fit in nicely with a political campaign against the industry waged by Cesar Chavez of the United Farm Workers.

More recently, we were informed about a *Cagney and Lacey* program about death squads from El Salvador working in New York City. One viewer said the program made it appear as though the death squads were working with some shadowy U.S. Government agency. The story line was apparently taken from a group called the U.S. Committee in Solidarity with the People of El Salvador, or CISPES. CISPES, a pro-communist organization, made headlines last year by claiming that Salvadoran death squads were operating on the West Coast. CISPES even produced witnesses who claimed to have been harassed or tortured by the death squads. But there was strong doubt that they were true. First of all, most of the so-called witnesses were members of CISPES. Second, real victims of death squads don't live to tell about it. And finally, government officials denounced the claims as a publicity stunt.

Cagney and Lacey is supposed to be drama. But it's becoming increasingly clear that it is being used as a vehicle for introducing leftist propaganda into the home under the guise of entertainment. This seems to be a deliberate effort on the part of those involved in the show.

May 3, 1988

103

Veteran TV Journalist Blasts Network News

Liz Trotta tells how liberals control what gets on the air

The February 27 issue of *TV Guide* magazine carried a scorching criticism of the decline in journalistic standards in the TV network news departments. The article was not by a professional media critic. It was by Liz Trotta, a veteran TV journalist who spent 20 years in the business, covering the world for NBC and CBS News. She was the first female TV war correspondent in Vietnam, and her last assignment as a war correspondent was covering the U.S. rescue operation in Grenada in 1983. The title of her *TV Guide* article is *Why the Network Didn't Want My Exclusive on Grenada*.

The network she refers to was CBS. The exclusive was information she had gathered from both the officers who commanded the operation and civilian contacts about new details of what had transpired, what had gone wrong, and why the operation had been undertaken in the first place. A senior producer had tried to get the story on the air, but nothing happened. Three weeks later, the producer called saying, "You'd better read *The Wall Street Journal* this morning. Your story is on the front page." What the network had not found worth reporting had finally become national news three weeks later.

Instead of airing the exclusive news story that Liz Trotta had dug up, using reportorial skills she had learned as a newspaper and wire service reporter, CBS sent down a few of its "stars" to do on-camera reports on the operation for the CBS *Evening News*. Trotta says that TV news has fallen victim to the cult of the personality. She says that today the networks want performers, not reporters. They draw their staffs from the ranks of the local stations, where, she says, "on-air people are cute as buttons, finish every sentence with a show of teeth and consider knowing how to write an optional skill.''

When Trotta broke into TV news in 1966, reporters for NBC were required to have five years experience with a major or medium-sized newspaper. They had to pass a writing test. Today they are auditioned by video cassette, and it is often impossible to tell if they even wrote the story they have submitted for their audition.

Trotta says that the network star system was perfected by a former CBS News president, Van Gordon Sauter, who said he wanted "gut-wrenching, sensational moments to lure the viewer into every story." He gave top priority to the trial of socialite Claus von Bulow, who was accused of trying to murder his wealthy wife. He assigned 14 people to cover that trial. Trotta told a colleague who was covering the fighting in El Salvador who couldn't get his stories on the air that he might do better if he tried to get a Salvadoran reaction to the von Bulow verdict.

Trotta says that TV news has been taken over by an elite group of "movers and shakers" who view the world from "the insulated premises of country houses, fancy restaurants and chauffeured limousines." Liz Trotta was one of the speakers at the recent Conservative Political Action Conference in Washington. She was asked if it was possible for an able conservative reporter to rise to the top in TV network news. After a long pause she said, "Unless he really keeps his mouth shut, probably not." Why? Because TV network news is run by and for limousine liberals.

March 11, 1988

PBS Program Trashes The Grenada Rescue Operation

Seymour Hersh on program 'Operation Urgent Fury' misleads on U.S. rescue

On February 2, the night President Reagan made his speech appealing to the nation to continue support for the anticommunist freedom fighters in Nicaragua, our tax-payer supported *Public Broadcasting Service* (PBS) tried to undercut the President's message. Like ABC, CBS and NBC, it refused to alter its regular schedule and have its stations air the President's speech and the Democratic response live. Instead it aired a program about the frozen remains of three British sailors who died in an expedition to the Arctic in 1845.

Following that, PBS aired a documentary titled *Operation Urgent Fury*, which conveyed the message that our 1983 military operation to rescue the 600 American students on the Caribbean Island of Grenada was both badly bungled and unjustified. Nicaragua wasn't mentioned, but the program appeared to us to have a bearing on the upcoming debate in Congress on aid to the Nicaraguan freedom fighters. If we had no business interfering with the communist control of Grenada and if we badly misjudged the threat the communists there posed to our national security, it could be inferred that we were making the same mistake in supporting the Nicaraguan freedom fighters.

The reporter for this PBS documentary was Seymour Hersh, a leftist reporter formerly with *The New York Times*. In a talk he gave in 1986, Hersh described the landing of American troops on Grenada as "one of the worst days this nation, as a superpower, has" had. He called the reaction "jingoism," and said it was sad that Grenada had been

106

accepted as a foreign policy triumph. That was essentially the same message that Hersh put into the PBS documentary.

It was argued in the film that we really knew very little about what was happening on Grenada. The president, it was said, was wrong in suggesting that Grenada posed any threat to our national security. The big airfield being built by the Cubans was just for tourism, not for military use. Maurice Bishop, the communist prime minister, was trying to improve relations with the U.S., but he failed because of our hostility.

The film totally ignored the wealth of documents that we captured on Grenada that refuted these arguments. These documents showed that Bishop and his colleagues were totally dedicated to promoting the interests of Cuba and the Soviet Union. External indications to the contrary were nothing but ploys to deceive non-communists in the West. Greg Sandford, who studied the documents and wrote a book based on them, said Grenada "acted consciously as an agent of world revolution. . . It offered Grenada as a training ground and safe haven for that purpose." He found that the airfield lacked sound economic justification and that military use was intended.

Hersh downplayed the terror that gripped Grenada in October 1983 when Bishop, his close supporters and an uncounted number of civilians were killed in a bloody power struggle. He found an American student who didn't think the students were in danger, but the great majority showed by their actions that they were extremely grateful to the troops and to President Reagan for rescuing them. Hersh also ignored the fact that a CBS poll showed that 90 percent of the Grenadian people felt the same way.

March 3, 1988

FBI
Fights For
Equal Time

TV networks try to hurt FBI on CISPES investigation

The FBI took a beating in the media over charges that it improperly or perhaps illegally investigated a group called the Committee in Solidarity with the People of El Salvador (CISPES). ABC News made the individual making the charges its "Person of the Week." It hailed Margaret Ratner of the Center for Constitutional Rights as someone who did "good for all Americans" and who defended individual rights. But the media gave far less attention to the FBI's rebuttal of the charges. In fact, the media continued their cover-up of the true nature of CISPES.

All three network news programs emphasized that FBI Director William Sessions had acknowledged that some FBI agents may have gone too far in handling the investigation. ABC News law correspondent Tim O'Brien's report showed FBI critic Congressman Don Edwards of California complaining about Sessions' defense of the probe. Edwards said Sessions was starting out with the wrong attitude by whitewashing the actions of the bureau.

But the whitewash was by O'Brien and other reporters who ignored the information that Sessions and other FBI officials provided about the nature of CISPES and its links to the Communist terrorists in El Salvador. Sessions said the investigation was narrow in focus and examined charges that the group was involved in illegal support of the Salvadoran guerrillas. Reporters were provided with an excerpt of a House Intelligence Committee hearing showing that CISPES had been organized by agents of the Communist Party of El Salvador, the Communist Party USA, and representatives of the Cuban mission to the United Nations. But none of this information was reported by the three networks, or *The New York Times* and *The Washington Post*.

The Post story about Sessions' rebuttal referred to CISPES as just a liberal group. It described the Communists in El Salvador as just the "leftist opposition." There was a slight change, however, at *The New York Times*. Reporter Philip Shenon, who had described CISPES as liberal in his initial story, acknowledged in his story about Sessions that it was actually "sympathetic" to the goals of the Communist guerrillas. In publicizing the initial charges, the media had made it appear that groups like the United Auto Workers and the National Education Association had also been targets of investigation. But Sessions said these groups came under scrutiny only because members of CISPES had made contact with them. The focus, he said, remained on CISPES. ABC's Peter Jennings said the closing of the investigation meant that the FBI had failed to uncover a threat to national security. That is definitely not the case. CISPES remains a major potential threat to national security because of its close and open association with the Communist guerrillas of El Salvador, who have murdered U.S. military advisers in the country. In fact, on February 20 these guerrillas announced a new plan to eliminate those advisers.

The closing of the investigation only means that the FBI was unable to develop enough evidence to take to court, or that the laws regulating with foreign communist powers need to be tightened up. There's no indication that CISPES has discontinued its practice of sending aid to the Salvadoran guerrillas.

March 2, 1988

ABC's Political Statement

ABC program "Weekend War" used to turn public against U.S. involvement in Central America

The Administration's defeat on aid to the Nicaraguan freedom fighters can be blamed in part on the unprecedented decision by the three broadcasting networks to censor President Reagan's speech to the nation in favor of such aid. ABC's censorship of the president was especially obvious because one night earlier the network aired a movie called *Weekend War*, which constituted a two-hour commercial against U.S. involvement in Central America.

The fictional movie told the story of American civilians who went to Honduras for National Guard duty only to get involved in a conflict on the Nicaraguan border. Some of the guardsmen returned home to their grieving relatives in coffins draped with American flags. One of the actors, Charles Haid, said, *"Weekend War* is probably the most courageous attempt by a network to take a stand. The thing that's fascinating about this entire event is that they made a very specific film with a very specific message about our involvement in Central America. . . ABC has actually made a major political statement. The film they came up with asks the question: What are we doing in Central America?"

In real life the training of the National Guard in Central America has become a hot political issue. Democratic presidential candidate Michael Dukakis, who is governor of Massachusetts, has filed suit to prevent the training of his state National Guard in Central America. Dukakis is also a strong critic of Reagan Administration policy in the region, including support for the Nicaraguan freedom fighters.

In addition, radical groups around the country have tried

110

to make National Guard training in Central America a political issue. So-called peace demonstrators have staged protests outside National Guard armories, claiming that the guard has been engaged in the "militarization" of the region.

In reality, the Guard trains in Honduras and 57 other countries. No Guard member participating in any exercise has ever been involved in an armed conflict or hostile situation. Three guardsmen have died in Central America; one died in a swimming accident, two others died when their helicopter developed a mechanical problem and crashed. But no members of the Guard died after being shot or wounded by hostile forces. The ABC movie shows the guardsmen being killed after being instructed to build an airfield and a bridge. The building of the bridge was said to be the pet project of a General in the Pentagon. In fact, Guard units are not building airfields, and they operate under supervision of the executives and legislative branches of government. The Guard says its activities have been covered by more than 1,200 national and international journalists, and not one has reported anything that resembles the scenario described in the ABC movie.

Officers in the National Guard were outraged by the ABC movie. One official said, "It is nothing more than a political statement by the network and the producer. It supports their political agenda but in no way reflects the facts and reality of National Guard training. . . ABC has betrayed the public trust by suggesting that the viewer consider or make a decision on our foreign and military policy based on a totally distorted and fictionalized scenario."

February 19, 1988

111

NBC Protects Gorbachev

Network edits Gorbachev speech to mislead on its true meaning

The issue of U.S.-Soviets relations is probably the most important of our time. In order to make an informed judgment about how to deal with the Soviets, the American people need to be given all the facts regarding Soviet ruler Mikhail Gorbachev's ambitions and goals. If, for example, Gorbachev believes in a one-world communist state, in which the American way of life would be destroyed, it would seem that the American media have an obligation to report that to the public.

But in a dangerous display of journalistic arrogance, an NBC vice president, Stephen Stander, has defended the editing of a Gorbachev speech in a way that made it appear as though the Soviet ruler had given up his goal of world communism. The editing occurred on the NBC *Nightly News* on November 2 in a report by Moscow correspondent Sandy Gilmour on Gorbachev's speech commemorating the 70th anniversary of communism in the Soviet Union.

Gorbachev concluded the speech by saying, "We are moving towards a new world, the world of communism. We shall never turn off that road." But Gilmour simply said that "Gorbachev concluded that the Soviet Union was moving towards a new world."

The difference between what Gilmour reported and what Gorbachev actually said is enormous. The report that the Soviets are moving towards a new world sounds perfectly innocent and defensible. The statement that they are moving towards a world of communism suggests a one-world com-

112

munist state in which Western democracies such as the United States are destroyed.

In excusing Gilmour's distorted report, Stander claims as fact that the speech was concerned with "the realization of Communist goals within the Soviet Union—not world domination." According to his logic, Gorbachev's closing statement about a world of communism is a reference to internal politics. This is ridiculous on its face.

Even granting that is the case, however, Gorbachev made several other references to the world communist movement. He said, for example, that "the choice between socialism and capitalism is the main social alternative of our epoch. . . " Addressing his "comrades," including Communist Party USA general secretary Gus Hall, Gorbachev said, "The world communist movement grows and develops upon the soil of each of the countries concerned. . . "

And the Soviet ruler favorably reflected on the activities of the Communist International, which was formed to export Communist revolution by establishing communist parties and organizations around the world. Gorbachev said the Communist International "is part of our movement's great past." He said the movement "has turned into a school of internationalism and revolutionary brotherhood. It has made internationalism an effective instrument furthering the interests of the working people and promoting the social progress of big and small nations."

Stander is certainly entitled to his interpretation of Gorbachev's speech, as ignorant as it is. He either didn't read it or read it selectively.

But Gilmour's deceptive editing of the speech, by cutting Gorbachev off in mid-sentence, is something else. This cannot be defended.

January 25, 1988

113

The Dishonesty
of Bill Moyers

Moyers, on PBS documentary, "God and Politics"

Bill Moyers' PBS documentary, *God and Politics*, posed the question of whether the role of the church should be to save souls or to change society. To present this as a debate within the Christian churches, Moyers contrasted the role being played by evangelical missionaries in Honduras with American advocates of liberation theology working in Nicaragua. The former were saving souls by preaching the gospel and trying to change people "from the inside out." The latter were planting trees and building water systems, while singing the praises of the Marxist-Leninist revolution in Nicaragua and condemning the United States for opposing it.

The way Moyers presented the debate, the liberation theologists, the Marxists, seemed to come out the winners. Moyers virtually declared himself to be on their side at the conclusion of the program, saying that charity, which the evangelicals had been shown dispensing, was like a drop of water on a parched lip, but that justice, which the liberation theologists claimed to be bringing to the poor, was like a water system that is there long after.

But Bill Moyers showed his dishonesty in the way he presented the debate. He took for granted the claims of the liberation theologists that they knew how to change society for the better. No one disputes that planting trees and building water systems improves the environment and living conditions, but that is not what liberation theology is all about. It is based on the premise that the entire social structure needs to be revolutionized along Marxist lines. Power and property must be taken from the rich and successful and distributed to the poor and unsuccessful. Salvation, according to this doctrine, lies in socialism.

The fact is that the socialism of the Sandinistas has caused greater misery and poverty in Nicaragua than existed under the previous regime. The economy is in a mess, and not only food, but even water is in short supply in Managua. That helps explain why hundreds of thousands of Nicaraguans have fled their country and why some 20,000 poor campesinos have joined the freedom fighters and taken up arms to get rid of the Sandinista dictatorship.

Bill Moyers must know that the economic and social system advocated by the liberation theologists has not brought abundance, equality or liberty to the poor people in any country in which it has been tried. This is a critical point in any debate about the merits of liberation theology, but it was totally ignored in the Moyers documentary. Indeed, Moyers who had shown many scenes of poverty in Honduras when he was talking about the evangelical missionaries, did not dwell on poverty and the manifest failures of the Nicaraguan revolution when he presented the case of the liberation theologists in Nicaragua.

The opponents of liberation theology are not merely evangelical Christians and the arguments against it are not purely theological. Its opponents are Christians, Jews and nonbelievers alike who understand that Marxism disguised as religion is no more a solution to man's problems than is Marxism pure and undiluted. That was the issue Moyers dishonestly ducked in his December 9 documentary on PBS.

January 22, 1988

PBS Blames World Hunger On America

PBS program, "The Politics of Hunger" claims U.S. is causing starvation throughout the world

A year ago the *Public Broadcasting Service* was busily engaged in warding off an independent investigation of its programming practices in the area of public affairs. The Corporation for Public Broadcasting, which doles out taxpayer dollars to PBS and to public television stations, was threatening to fund a scholarly analysis to check on the validity of complaints that PBS documentaries were predominantly left-liberal. PBS got its friends in Congress to pressure CPB to call off the dogs. It set up its own in-house investigation to produce a report that would demonstrate that the charges of leftist bias were without foundation.

The PBS investigating committee made no analysis of the programs, but that didn't deter it from concluding that everything was just fine. It said that PBS had "encouraged programs of high quality that reflect a wide range of information, opinion and artistic expression and that satisfy accepted journalistic standards." The committee added that there should be a periodic review to see that PBS is encouraging "quality, integrity and diversity."

In view of the performance of PBS since that report was published last spring, the time has come for somebody to undertake that periodic review, preferably not one under the control of PBS. A congressional committee would be ideal. The trouble is that very few members of Congress evidently watch public television documentaries, and so they don't know how bad they can be.

This was disclosed recently when one congressman brought up a particularly outrageous documentary, Bill Moyers' *The Secret Government. . . The Constitution in Crisis*, at a meeting of the Republican members of Congress. He found it difficult to get them to share his indignation over the fact that big taxpayer bucks had been squandered on this one-sided, left-wing program. Why? Because none of them had seen it. If Congress would conduct an investigation of PBS programming practices, a lot of our representatives might finally learn something about how the millions of dollars they appropriate for public broadcasting each year are actually spent.

Take the matter of encouraging diversity. PBS always says it believes in diversity, but it has always had trouble finding acceptable documentaries of a political nature that don't have a leftist slant. That's what they say, but they are notorious for finding anti-communist documentaries "unacceptable." We saw this again this year when efforts were made to get public television to air two excellent Canadian documentaries. One, *Agents of Deception*, was a fascinating exposé of the disinformation operations of the Soviet Union. The other, *Angola*, covered the conflict in Angola from the standpoint of the UNITA forces under Jonas Savimbi.

Both films were professionally done and covered important topics of current interest. Neither could get the PBS imprimatur. Both were finally acquired by the South Carolina Educational Television System, which offered them to other public television stations via the PBS satellite. No one knows how many stations actually aired them.

In contrast to this, PBS on December 29, aired *The Politics of Hunger*, a British documentary that tried to demonstrate that the United States and its wicked capitalists were responsible for starvation throughout the world. This film heavily featured comments from American left-wingers. One was Susan George, identified as a fellow of the Institute of Policy Studies. That's a far-left think tank in Washington. Another was Frances Moore Lappe.

In 1982 Lappe co-authored a book singing the praises of the Sandinista revolution in Nicaragua. She has also extolled the land reform policies in Vietnam and Cuba, but in the PBS documentary on hunger, none of these countries was men-

117

tioned, since their agricultural results have been very disappointing. Famine-ridden Marxist Ethiopia was also ignored. PBS put its logo on this documentary and gave it two hours of prime time. It brazenly blamed us for world hunger and ignored the disasters caused by the Marxists. This program failed the tests of quality, integrity and plain common sense.

January 8, 1988

A Reporter's
Source
Is Blown

How a rumor gets printed as fact

A year ago, while the media were having the most fun
since Watergate with the story of the Iran arms sales, *The
New York Times* came out with a big front-page story reporting allegations that some of the profits from the arms sales
had been used to support the election campaigns of conservative candidates running for the House and Senate. This was
supposed to have been done by Col. North giving the money
to a private fundraiser named Spitz Channel. The story was
based on a report published in a small Massachusetts daily,
The Lowell Sun. It was written by their Washington correspondent, Tom Squitieri.

Squitieri's story, which claimed that $5 million was
involved, excited the networks as well as *The New York
Times*. People wondered how it happened that a reporter for a
small-town paper could break the most damning story yet
published about the Iran arms affair. Squitieri became famous
overnight. Reporters for *The New York Times* and other big
papers immediately began scrambling to find credible sources
who could confirm the story. Squitieri insisted that he had
good sources, but they had to be kept confidential.

The day after it splashed the damaging allegations on the
front page, *The New York Times* ran a second story, also on
page one. It was about Spitz Channel and his links to the
White House. But the second paragraph was really the reason
for the story's appearance. It disclosed that The Times had
been unable to find any evidence to support the charge that
funds had been diverted into political campaigns as Squitieri
had reported. An aide to the Senate Intelligence committee
was quoted as saying there had been no hint of any such

diversion in all the evidence assembled. The story had fizzled out, but Tom Squitieri still stood by it.

Nearly one year later, *The City Paper*, a Washington, D.C. weekly, published a story telling how Squitieri discovered his great scoop. Carol Matlack, who was then a reporter for *The Gazette* of Little Rock, Arkansas, had heard rumors that Channel had diverted funds obtained from Col. North into political campaigns. Some liberal members of Congress suspected this had happened. Miss Matlack checked out these suspicions with some of the members of Congress or Congressional aides, but she could find no one who had any evidence. On Friday, December 12, Matlack described her unsuccessful efforts to check out the allegation to her friend Squitieri.

Matlack told *The City Paper* that she was stunned to see in *The New York Times* the following Monday an article about the alleged fund diversion based on a story that Squitieri had in *The Lowell Sun* the day before. She said that it appeared to her that she was the main source for Squitieri's story. She said, "A story had gone all over the world which I believed was wrong."

When Matlack saw Squitieri, she chided him, saying, "You've taken this rumor and printed it as fact." She said Squitieri insisted that he had been able to check out the story through two unnamed sources at the National Security Council, but that claim lacks credibility. But instead of being disgraced, Squitieri found a job with a bigger paper, *The Boston Herald*.

December 8, 1987

The Politics Of Perry Mason

Entertainment program is used to send message not to trust military

Years ago, in a book called *The View From Sunset Boulevard*, Ben Stein documented the politics of America's entertainment community. He found that Hollywood producers and writers had, among other things, biases against business people and the military which were reflected in the programs they put on the air. The importance of that book was renewed once again when NBC aired a Perry Mason movie on November 15th called *The Case of the Scandalous Scoundrel*. This movie was unlike some of the old Perry Mason episodes. This was a carefully orchestrated attack on anti-communists and the military. It even included a swipe at our Central America policy.

Perry Mason is the lawyer who defends a former reporter for a sleazy tabloid called *The Confidential Informer*. She is charged with murdering her former editor. She was fired from the paper after complaining about having to write what are called "smear jobs" of prominent people. The editor also likes sensationalism, as evidenced by his approval for publication of a story about someone kidnapped by Martians from outer space. The reporter asked to write a story about bad conditions in a nursing home for old people, but the editor didn't want that in his paper. At one point he boasts that his paper specializes in "kicking the (blank) out of Commie-loving politicians."

Anti-communism is thus portrayed as a publicity gimmick, as a sleazy tactic used to generate sales of a sensationalistic tabloid. It's implied that stories about "Commie-loving politicians" are in the same class as "smear jobs" and stories about aliens from Mars. Such dialogue in a major television movie is not an accident. It's a deliberate effort to plant political ideas in the minds of those who watch it.

It turns out, of course, that the honest reporter concerned about abuse of the elderly did not commit the murder. The killer is a former military man who was afraid that the sleazy editor would publish a damaging story about his associate, General Sorenson, who is said to have been involved in a scandal during the Vietnam War. The program thus reinforced the sterotype of veterans of that war being corrupt or deranged.

Before Perry Mason actually nails the real killer, he takes a trip out to visit General Sorenson, who seems to be supervising war games somewhere. There are scenes of soldiers running around and shooting their weapons. It soon becomes apparent that the general is some kind of military nut who gets a kick from guns. Beyond that, it appears the general is either a mercenary or an operative of the U.S. Government. When Perry Mason asks what the soldiers are training for, the general replies, "they'll probably wind up in Central America."

The viewer is obviously supposed to think back to the Iran arms affair and all of the charges and stories about American support for the Nicaraguan resistance. The messages of this Perry Mason movie were simple ones: don't trust the military, and don't believe stories about politicians being soft on communism. In fact, we should fear our own military more than the communists.

December 1, 1987

No Thank You, Paine Webber

Bill Moyers' mendacious propaganda on Guatemala and U.S. intervention is supported by brokerage

In our previous broadcast we pointed out that a recent PBS documentary, narrated by Bill Moyers, had advocated that the United States quit using covert operations to combat communist aggression and subversion. Moyers argued that the CIA and other intelligence operatives constitute a secret government that tramples on our laws and creates a constitutional crisis. This totally onesided program not only ignored the legal requirement that programs funded with federal tax dollars be balanced, but it was also riddled with errors and distortions.

For example, in condemning successful CIA covert operations to overthrow the president of Guatemala in 1954, Moyers derided the claim that this had to be done to prevent the establishment of a Soviet beachhead in Central America. He described the president, Jacobo Arbenz, as an admirer of Franklin Roosevelt who wanted merely to bring a Roosevelt-like New Deal to Guatemala. He presented a retired Marine colonel who assured the viewers that there was not even a hint of communism in the Arbenz government.

What Moyers omitted was the fact that Arbenz had been elected as Guatemala's president after his anti-communist opponent, Francisco Arana, was assassinated. The car carrying the death squad belonged to Mrs. Arbenz and was driven by her chauffeur. The leader of the death squad was a close friend of Arbenz's, who was subsequently rewarded with a promotion and became Arbenz's personal secretary when he assumed the presidency.

Moyers also neglected to point out that the two top communist leaders in Guatemala were close friends and advisers to president Arbenz. He didn't mention that Arbenz acknowledged to the American ambassador that there were communists in his government and that government advertising was used to support the Communist Party newspaper. Moyers overlooked the fact that Mrs. Arbenz was known as a Communist. She defended the memorial observance of the death of Soviet dictator Josef Stalin by the Guatemalan Congress.

The far left programs of the Arbenz regime were ruining the Guatemalan economy, and the anti-communists were experiencing a reign of terror. The U. S. decided that Arbenz was a threat to the security of the Western Hemisphere, and the CIA helped organize a small army of Guatemalan exiles to invade the country. It provided them with air support, which was decisive in persuading the Guatemalan army to withdraw its support of Arbenz. Bloodshed was minimal.

Moyers presented this as an American intervention in Guatemalan affairs that had no justification. He did it by omitting vital important facts. He did the same thing in discussing Iran and Vietnam, showing himself to be a master of misrepresentation.

This propaganda, which must have delighted the KGB, cost $625,000, of which $375,000 came from the taxpayers. The remaining $250,000 was a gift from Paine Webber, the stock brokers famous for the commercials that end with the words, "Thank you, Paine Webber." For foisting this mendacious Moyers propaganda on the nation, Paine Webber deserves no thanks from the American people.

November 19, 1987

Soviet Scientists Denounce KGB Disinformation

How Dan Rather spread Soviet disinformation about AIDS being started by U.S.

Two years ago, the Soviet Union began spreading the story that the AIDS virus had been created in a U.S. Army biological warfare laboratory and had spread from there around the world. A year later the story made front-page headlines in *The Express*, a major British daily paper. It had been publicized not only in the Iron Curtain countries, but also in Africa, where AIDS is widespread and where pinning the blame on the United States could do us a lot of harm. A year ago, the State Department fought back, giving a special press briefing exposing this story as Soviet disinformation.

The reporters present at that briefing largely treated the story as a joke. They didn't take it seriously, and they assumed that no one else would. Very little publicity was given to the proof that this was soviet disinformation. Even the Associated Press ignored the story.

The Soviets were therefore not deterred from pushing their disinformation campaign. They kept publicizing the charge that the U.S. Army was responsible for creating the AIDS virus. One of these articles came to the attention of CBS News. On March 30 of this year, Dan Rather solemnly told his viewers on the CBS *Evening News* that a Soviet military publication had reported that the AIDS virus was the product of a U.S. Army biological warfare laboratory. Rather said that the article offered no hard evidence, but it claimed to be reporting the conclusions of unnamed scientists in the United States, Britain and East Germany.

Dan Rather had evidently not heard that the State Department had exposed this as disinformation five months earlier.

CBS News didn't bother to check with the Defense Department or the State Department to see if they had any comment on the Soviet charge. It simply put the story on the air without trying to find out the true facts. In doing so, it gave increased credibility to the Soviet charge. The result is that there is now some evidence that even in this country some people believe the charge is true, according to the State Department.

CBS News has rejected all demands that they do something to set the record straight. At first, there was some ambiguity in their responses. It seemed that some of their officials thought the Soviet charges might be true, but the president of CBS News, Howard Stringer, eventually said they knew it was disinformation and admitted that their broadcast might not have made that clear.

On October 30, CBS was presented with a golden opportunity to set the record straight. *The Washington Times* carried a report from Moscow saying that top Soviet scientists had told a news conference that "not a single serious scientist has even hinted that AIDS was artificially manufactured." Space expert Roald Sagdeev said the Soviet Academy of Sciences had never had anything to do with such accusations. Academician Vitaly Goldansky said the claim was typical of groundless sensationalism by journalists. He said he always protested the publication of such statements.

CBS News, which had helped spread this "groundless sensationalism" apparently missed the denunciation by the Soviet scientists. It didn't report their statements to its viewers.

November 17, 1987

126

Soviet Star Wars Don't Excite Our Media

Media don't report how Soviets are building missile defense

Suppose the U. S. military were building an installation on the Rocky Mountains that could send powerful laser beams into space to destroy orbiting satellites or nuclear warheads. Would this be kept secret from the American people? No way. *The New York Times* and *The Washington Post* would run headline stories. Editorials would denounce our violations of the ABM treaty by our reckless pursuit of "star wars." The TV networks would run to show aerial photos of the complex along with protest demonstrations led by such celebrities as Jane Fonda, Ed Asner and Martin Sheen.

We reported last week that our government has been monitoring the construction of a giant weapons laser complex on a mountain top in the Soviet Union near the city of Dushanbe, near the Afghan border. This became known when photos of the complex taken by a French satellite were sold to news organizations around the world. One of these photos was printed in *The New York Times* on October 23 and was also aired by ABC News. It showed ten domes housing the lasers and the tracking equipment, a control center, headquarters and support buildings and a power station. Experts said this was definitely a military installation and that the lasers are the largest built to date.

Although our military satellites have been photographing this "star wars" complex as construction proceeded, the American people have not been previously informed about what the Soviets are up to. Even now, we can only guess. Are these powerful laser weapons intended to shoot down American satellites? We have been told that the Soviets have already deployed lasers that can knock out or damage satellites orbiting at altitudes as high as 750 miles. We have also been told that within five years they will be able to destroy or damage our geosynchronous satellites that are stationed 22,300 miles above the equator.

What we don't know is if these new lasers are capable of destroying nuclear warheads in space. Are they perhaps linked to the huge radar at Krasnoyarsk, which our government believes is designed to help defend against incoming ballistic missiles, in violation of the ABM treaty?

There has been remarkably little concern shown by our media about the new Soviet laser complex, even though it suggests that the Soviets may be farther along in the development of a strategic defense against nuclear missiles than we are. *The New York Times* ran a good story about it, but it was buried deep inside the paper. *The Washington Post* ignored it altogether, as did CBS News. The editorial board of *The New York Times* perhaps didn't see the story or missed its significance. Ten days after the story appeared, The Times ran an editorial expressing the hope that President Reagan would limit work on the SDI.

The fact that our own government is helping the Soviets keep secret the strides they are making in deploying "star wars" type technology such as weapons lasers concerns Dr. Edward Teller. He is the physicist who sold Reagan on the need for an antimissile defense. Dr. Teller can't understand why it is necessary for the Defense Department to keep the Dushanbe laser complex secret. If the American people knew that the Soviets were getting the jump on us, they would be far more likely to support speedy development of our own "star wars" technology.

November 11, 1987

No
Right
To Know

Press corps neglects news at press conferences to shout
questions designed to embarrass the President

Members of the White House press corps have been making fools of themselves by shouting questions at the president
of the United States. On September 18th, after the president
told a White House briefing that he was on the verge of an
arms agreement with the Soviets, reporters such as Sam Donaldson of ABC, Bill Plante of CBS, and Chris Wallace of
NBC tried to outshout each other with questions. This went
on for about 15 seconds and because nobody could hear the
questions the president joked that he needed an interpreter.

On October 5th, after a ceremony in honor of American
educators, reporters once again shouted at the president. But
the teachers and principals didn't treat that as a joke. They
chastised Donaldson and Plante as if they were naughty
school children. They accused the reporters of trying to ruin
their ceremony. In turn, Donaldson and Plante criticized the
educators, telling them that the First Amendment applied in
the Rose Garden and they were only trying to get information.

Donaldson, Plante and others have tried to justify this
obnoxious behavior by claiming that the president has not
been accessible to the press. What they really mean is that the
president has not been appearing at nationally televised news
conferences as often as they would like. These are events at
which reporters can try to embarrass or humiliate the
president.

It's a matter of opinion if the president has held enough
news conferences. It is also a matter of debate if the news
conference is the best way to get the president's views across
to the American people. What cannot be disputed is the fact

that the president has tried on several occasions to communicate to the public but has been censored. On October 14th, the three broadcast networks refused to carry a presidential speech to the nation in support of Supreme Court nominee Robert Bork. *The Washington Post* carried a story about the speech on page six and *The New York Times* carried its story about the speech on page D-31, the next to last page of the newspaper.

This isn't the first time his views have been censored or buried by a media that claims the public has a right to know. The networks have not reported the president's statements that Communist disinformation activities have affected the Congress and the media. These statements were reported by *The Washington Times* at a time when the president was supposedly inaccessible to the press. These remarks were the subject of several questions at a White House press briefing, but were not reported to the American people by the network news programs.

The failure of Sam Donaldson and company to cover those statements shows they are less interested in getting information out of the president than in promoting themselves at a news conference or trying to embarrass the president. An example of this occurred last March when the president signed a proclamation at the White House marking American support for the Afghan freedom fighters. The reporters in attendance weren't interested in the cause of freedom in Afghanistan. After the ceremony ended, they began asking the president questions about the Iran arms affair. Senator Gordon Humphrey, who was there with the president, scolded the press for its narrow and short-sighted view. His example should be followed by others. The public deserves better from the press corps.

October 29, 1987

130

NBC Promotes Teen-Age Homosexuality

A one-sided program spreads incorrect information

Last March the CBS television network enraged parents across the country with a program directed at kids called, *What if I'm Gay?* It told students that homosexuality is a normal lifestyle and they don't have to worry about catching AIDS if they take precautions and get certain information. Now the NBC television network has gotten into the act. The NBC program for teenagers called *Mainstreet* recently aired a program that favorably profiled two "gay teenagers."

The tone was set by host Maria Shriver, who said, "Surveys estimate that about ten percent of all teenagers are homosexual. Scientists don't know why. Some think it's a combination of hormonal changes and experiences in early childhood. One thing they are sure of, however—homosexuality is not something homosexuals choose. It's just something they are or become. And they face a struggle because of it, often living in a harsh world of prejudice, sometimes even violence."

That is exactly what the homosexuals want people to believe. They want people to think they have no choice in the matter. However, it should be apparent that this is not necessarily the case, and that Shriver was incorrect when she claimed to speak for all of the scientific community on this issue. The truth is that choice is a factor in homosexuals who had freely given up their homosexuality.

The program noted on two occasions that not all people who experience homosexual feelings become homosexuals. But it did not point out that there is a lot of research indicating that free choice can play a role in that outcome. Aside from the research, there is evidence in the form of human beings

131

who have rejected homosexuality. Some of these people have formed organizations like Homosexuals Anonymous, based in Reading, Pennsylvania, which is modeled after Alcoholics Anonymous.

By portraying homosexuality as something, like blackness, that cannot be helped, the program played into the hands of the organized homosexual lobby that wants its members treated like other minority groups and given preferential treatment. This entails using the full force of government, through passage of a gay rights bill, to compel people to associate with open homosexuals in employment, housing and other areas of life. It should be no surprise that the *Washington Blade*, a homosexual newspaper in the nation's capital, found nothing to criticize in the program and that the program was itself prepared in collaboration with the so-called "homosexual community."

This was confirmed to us by the program's chief correspondent, Bill Sheckner, after we pressed him on the matter. He said, "We spoke with groups of people who are part of what I guess you'd call the homosexual community." When we asked for the names of those groups, he said, "I don't think I want to be interrogated." It is therefore possible that the "gay teens featured in the program were selected by the North American Man-Boy Love Association or some other group of pedophiles. Perhaps the most harmful cover-up was the failure of the program to warn those considering homosexuality that this so-called lifestyle is dangerous to human health and can cause death.

October 26, 1987

Bob Woodward Lies Again

Getting into Bill Casey's room at the hospital

Washington Post reporter and best-selling author Bob Woodward created a sensation with his claim that former CIA director William J. Casey had given him an interview as he lay dying at Georgetown University Hospital in January 1987. Woodward says in his new book, *Veil*, that he got into Casey's room in the intensive care ward at the hospital and interviewed the CIA chief about what he knew about the diversion of funds from the Iran arms sales to the Nicaraguan freedom fighters. He said Casey acknowledged with a nod that meant "yes" that he had known about the diversion all along.

Woodward had submitted this as a story to *The Washington Post* several months ago. The Post rejected it. Assistant managing editor Robert Kaiser has explained that the account was "too ambiguous." That's a polite way of saying that they didn't find it convincing. That didn't stop Woodward from including it as the final story in his new book, and it was the story that made the big headlines and the television news shows when the book was released at the end of September. *The Washington Post*, however, showed its mistrust of the story by burying it in the 17th paragraph of its big front-page story about the new book and its revelations. That was obviously not one of the revelations The Post thought deserved much attention.

Other editors, especially those in network television, didn't agree with the Post on that point. They featured the story, and it served to enhance the impression that Casey had spilled his guts to Woodward about a lot of other secrets as well. That is something that those who know Bill Casey well strongly doubt. There is overwhelming evidence that Bob Woodward is guilty of fabricating the story of his final interview with Bill Casey. If he lied about that, there is a high probability that he lied about a lot of other things in his book.

Three things prove that Woodward's claim that he visited Mr. Casey in the hospital and interviewed him is a fabrication.

First, there are the statements of Mrs. Casey, the widow of the CIA chief, and their daughter, Bernadette Casey Smith, that they personally maintained a 24-hour-a-day vigil at Mr. Casey's bedside during the entire time he was in the hospital. Mrs. Casey spent the nights there, and Mrs. Smith was there all day. They took their meals in the room and remained there in constant attendance. Both state categorically that Robert Woodward never entered the room and could not have done so without their knowledge.

Second, there is the fact that Woodward has given conflicting stories about how he got into the room. Adm. Standfield Turner, the CIA director in the Carter administration, stated on ABC's *Good Morning America* on September 30, that Woodward told him several months ago that he simply went to the room, found it unprotected by any guard and that Mr. Casey waved to him to come in. Woodward told Ryan Murphy of the Knight-Ridder papers last August that "he just showed his press pass and walked in." But in a *60 Minutes* segment that aired on September 27, Woodward refused to say what time of day the interview took place, saying, "Obviously somebody helped me, and I'm protecting that person." Asked by Mike Wallace how he got past the guards, Woodward said, "CIA security is nothing difficult to get around."

Woodward went much further in protecting his alleged helper or helpers when he appeared on *Nightline* on October 1. Ted Koppel, the *Nightline* host, called attention to a drawing in the October 5 issue of *Newsweek* showing Woodward interviewing Casey in the hospital room. Casey was depicted sitting in an arm chair, his back to the window. Koppel asked if that was accurate.

Again Woodward declined to say, saying that he had

heard that efforts were being made to identify "the people" who helped him get into the room. He said those people had to be protected. He gave that as the reason for refusing to provide any description of the setting. A spokesman for *Newsweek* confirmed that its drawing had been based on a description provided by Woodward's staff. It also pointed out that the account of the conversation in Woodward's book is consistent with Casey being seated rather than lying down. Woodward wrote that when he accused Casey of knowing of the diversion of arms-sales profits to the freedom fighters, "his head jerked up hard," not a motion that he would make if he was lying down.

Ted Koppel could not see how describing Casey's condition would "point a finger in anyone's direction." Refusal to confirm that Casey was sitting up made no sense.

Finally Woodward's description of Casey's condition was totally at variance from that of persons familiar with Casey's condition in late January, when Woodward claims his visit took place.

Woodward said Casey had uttered the following 19 words: "Okay. . . better. . . no. You finished yet? It hurts. Oh. What you don't know. I'm gone. I believed. I believed." In addition, he grunted once and gave a nod which Woodward says meant "yes," when he accused him of knowing about the fund diversion.

Those who saw Casey at that time agree that he could not have carried on such a conversation. His right side was paralyzed, and Mrs. Casey says he could utter only monosyllables and those, with difficulty. His secretary said she couldn't understand what he was trying to say, that he could say a few words, but they were hard to understand. A doctor familiar with the case said that he was suffering from severe aphasia, a condition that left him unable to understand or reply to questions. He said he could only be heard by putting an ear to his lips.

Woodward evidently based his fabricated interview on reports that had appeared in the press that suggested that Casey was getting better and his speech was returning to normal. Robert Gates, the deputy director of the CIA, who visited Casey on January 28 to discuss his resignation, was quoted as saying that he was lucid but "couldn't talk that well." Mrs. Casey, who was present during that meeting, said her husband understood what was wanted but that he couldn't discuss the matter. When the letter of resignation was brought in two days later, she had to sign it for him.

Woodward also had a false impression of Casey's physical condition. Mrs. Casey said it was absurd to say that Casey waved to Woodward. She said he couldn't even hold a glass of water in his unparalyzed left hand, much less wave it.

She found the idea that he was sitting alone in his room when Woodward came in even more absurd. She said it took two men to get him out of bed, and when he was placed in a chair, he slumped. He could not stand unaided and he was never left alone, even when he was lying in bed. Mrs. Casey said of Woodward's claims, "It's a lie. Woodward never saw my husband. He never got in to speak to him. He couldn't speak to him if he wanted to."

Woodward's story is fiction comparable to Janet Cooke's 1980 *Washington Post* story about an eight-year-old heroin addict named "Jimmy." Woodward was responsible for that story as metropolitan editor of *The Washington Post* and he promoted the story, which won a Pulitzer Prize, even though several of his subordinates had good reason to believe that it was a fake. The Pulitzer Prize was returned after the Associated Press revealed that reporter Janet Cooke had falsified her academic credentials and the Post's editors were forced for the first time to check her story for accuracy. They found that "Jimmy" was a figment of Janet Cooke's imagination.

October 14, 1987

How The Liberals Use Their Media

Three examples which show liberal bias is nothing new

Empire, a new biography of CBS Chairman William S. Paley, provides some fascinating insights into how the liberals who have long dominated CBS have unblushingly used their positions to advance their own political agendas. Author Lewis J. Paper tells how Norman Lear's radically new program, *All in the Family*, came to be aired by CBS after ABC had rejected it.

Paper writes: "Sam Cohen, Lear's agent, telephoned Mike Dann (of CBS) one day in 1968 and said he had a business project to discuss. Cohen had picked his target well. He and Dann were both Democrats and both eager to focus public attention on the political and social issues then confronting the nation. 'I want you to see a program,' Cohen explained to the CBS executive, 'and tell me why it can't get on the air.' Dann reviewed the pilot and was immediately ecstatic." Paley, a Republican, didn't like the program. He thought it was coarse and vulgar, but he was won over, and *All in the Family* went on to become a great hit, all the while spreading Norman Lear's liberal views on social and political issues.

CBS News was equally subject to being used for political ends. Paper says this of some notoriously controversial film footage from Vietnam: "In 1965 a young reporter named Morley Safer sent back film of an American GI using a cigarette lighter to set fire to the thatched roof of a home in a Vietnamese village. The graphic pictures did more to undermine the moral base of American participation than hundreds of congressional speeches. Friendly (the president of CBS News) understood the significance of the report from the start. After satisfying himself that Safer's report was accurate,

137

Friendly agreed that it should be broadcast. The News Division president then sat at the phones himself to help handle the avalanche of protests as people called to complain about a news report that surely had to have been fabricated."

The report may not have been fabricated, but it was misleading. Safer gave the impression that this was wanton destruction of a harmless village. The village had been converted by the Viet Cong into a fortified center. The Marines who occupied it found 38 trenches, tunnels and prepared positions as well as 51 structures, which they destroyed. The hut Safer showed being burned covered a concrete basement connected to a tunnel complex. Put in that context, the destruction didn't seem senseless, but CBS didn't provide the context.

The next year, in 1966, Fred Friendly, the CBS News president who had approved airing Safer's footage, resigned when he was blocked from pre-empting regular daytime programs to air live the testimony of George F. Kennan, an opponent of the Vietnam War, before the Senate Foreign Relations Committee. He had already aired live the testimony of retired Army General James Gavin, another critic of the way the war was being fought.

Friendly had earlier arranged a luncheon to enable another war critic, columnist Walter Lippmann, to give William Paley the benefit of his views on the war. But even though Paley expressed agreement with Lippmann's anti-war views, he refused to go along with Friendly's plan to cover Kennan's testimony live, perhaps because of the cost. Friendly felt so strongly about this that he resigned in protest.

October 6, 1987

The Pope
As Media
Critic

How the media covered his criticism

The Pope let the media have it during a speech in Burbank, California, on September 15th. He attacked pornography and too much sex and violence in the media. He criticized distortion in the presentation of the news. He said news personnel have the obligation to avoid the manipulation of the truth for any reason. But he wasn't just attacking inaccurate news reporting; he was attacking the deliberate distortion of the news for ideological reasons.

The Pope could have been talking about coverage of his own speech. It was barely mentioned by only one of the evening news programs that night. The next day, only two of the three network news morning programs carried a report about it. And those stories did not fully report his message. ABC News reporter David Ensor mistakenly said the speech was only directed at Hollywood. NBC News reporter Bob Abernathy ignored the tough criticism leveled at his own profession.

However, Ensor's report on ABC was important because it revealed that Hollywood wants to continue with business as usual, despite what the Pope said. He reported that Hollywood liked the speech, but actor Ed Asner answered "no" when asked if it would change anything. Actor Charles Durning said, "We know what we should do, and whether we do it or not is something else."

Abernathy of NBC News said simply that the Pope had urged entertainment and news business leaders always to consider the effects of what they do. The Pope was shown saying, "You must ask yourselves if what you communicate is consistent with the full measure of human dignity." That's an

139

important statement, but it was definitely not the most powerful in the speech.

Speaking to a group that included talk show host Phil Donahue, the Pope said media manipulation takes place when "certain issues are deliberately passed over in silence in order that others may be unduly emphasized. It also occurs when information is altered or withheld so that society will be less able to resist the imposition of a given ideology." Another media figure on the list of those invited to hear the Pope was Robert Erburu, president of *Times-Mirror*, which publishes *The Los Angeles Times*. *The Washington Post* noted that the Pope's speech condemning gratuitous sex in the media came on the very day *The Los Angeles Times* carried a lead feature story titled, *The Last of the Blonde Bombshells - (the) Saga of (an) Ex-Sex Kitten*. It was not reported if Mr. Erburu showed up, or if he did, if he was squirming uncomfortably in his chair.

The Washington Post carried a good story about the Pope's speech. But it also carried a silly little story about how hard it has been for some members of the press to cover the Pope's American trip. The story cited the "skillful manipulation" of the press by the Vatican and complained that neither the Pope nor his press representative had been making himself available to the reporters covering the trip. It is really not necessary for that to happen for the American people to understand what the Pope is saying and what he stands for. All that is necessary is for the media to accurately and fully report what he says. *The New York Times* did this. It had a page one story about the speech and carried extended excerpts of what he said.

September 30, 1987

140

ABC
Smears The
Catholic Church

Faulty reporting on how the Church treats AIDS victims

The visit of Pope John Paul II to America has produced tremendous coverage of the Catholic Church and what it stands for. But some media have gotten it all wrong. On September 3rd, before the visit, ABC *World News Tonight* aired a particularly vicious attack. Reporter Betsy Aaron claimed the church "only reluctantly ministers to AIDS patients" because of the church's stand against homosexuality. The church was thus portrayed as uncaring and unsympathetic toward the victims of a deadly disease.

Aaron's statement was false. Carl Eifert, an information officer for the U.S. Catholic Conference, says the church's teaching is that victims of AIDS should be treated with the same warmth, comfort and love accorded victims of other diseases or accidents. He said the church does not discriminate against AIDS victims. He noted that Mother Teresa, who has come to epitomize the caring spirit of the church, has opened a hospice for AIDS patients in Washington, D.C. Aaron, of course, never mentioned that.

Aaron compounded this injustice against the church by then focusing on a quilt being put together by homosexuals in San Francisco with the names of AIDS victims. She said they hope to present it to the Pope when he's in America because "there is a message in this quilt for the church." That message, according to one of the people featured in the ABC report, is "Wake Up. . . and change the way you look at people who are gay and the way you treat people who have AIDS." Aaron asked, "If you could ask the Pope for one thing, what would it be?" He replied, "understanding and

141

love." The implication, again, is that the church and the Pope have no understanding or love for homosexuals.

Early in the report, Aaron glossed over the church's teaching on homosexuality. She said a church letter referring to homosexuality as "intrinsically evil" and homosexuals as disordered" amounted to what she called an "indictment." This made it sound as though the church was out to convict and imprison the homosexuals.

Archbishop John Quinn of San Francisco was permitted to say that the church doesn't reject homosexuals as persons but the behavior that they engage in. But this was countered by a so-called Catholic homosexual who said he was tired of being kicked around and treated as less than human by the church. Aaron never mentioned the biblical basis for the teachings of the church on this issue. There are many citations from the Bible that condemn homosexual behavior. Leviticus chapter 20, verses 13 and 14 states categorically, "If a man has intercourse with a man as with a woman, they both commit an abomination. They shall be put to death; their blood shall be upon their own hands."

The final shot came when Aaron closed her piece by airing a statement by Virginia Apuzzo, a lesbian. She directed her words at the Pope, saying, "John Paul, open yourself to the spirit that is within us. Christ would do no less." As those words were spoken, viewers were shown pictures of what Aaron had previously described as proud homosexual Catholics trying to reach their Pope. The report ended with the symbol of Jesus Christ on the cross.

September 22, 1987

142

CBS
Under
Attack

CBS decides to air "Garbage Pail Kids." Judy Price says
nothing is off limits

The National Federation for Decency has launched a
national campaign to get the CBS television network to cancel
a scheduled cartoon program aimed at children called *Garbage Pail Kids*. The program, which is supposed to debut
September 19th, is based on the vulgar and violent trading
cards of the same name. The cards feature cartoon characters
with physical abnormalities. According to one report, they
have become a rage among children but an outrage among
parents.

The program has united conservatives and liberals against
CBS. Joining the National Federation for Decency in its campaign against the network are two liberal television activists,
Peggy Charren of Action for Children's Television and Dr.
Thomas Radecki of the National Coalition on Television Violence. Charren says the CBS cartoon program promotes a
kind of humor that is mean and ghastly. Dr. Radecki says,
". . . by using anything that is related to the cards, (CBS is)
saying it's okay to get a laugh out of brutal sadism."

Kids can pick the cards up at drug stores and grocery
stores. Each cartoon character has a name and a description of
his or her particular physical problem. For example, one
shows a character named *Leaky Lindsay*. She is shown hold-
ing mucus that has drained out of her nose. Another character, *Dribblin Derek*, shows a basketball player dribbling his
detached head. Another, *Nailed Nell*, shows a girl on a bed of
nails with the nails protruding through her entire body.

Judy Price, CBS vice president for children's programming, defends the cartoon by saying that it won't use some of

the more sickening characters. Her program will feature some that are supposed to be milder, such as *Elliot Mess*, whose body parts are scrambled, and *Clogged Duane*, who can liquefy and slip down drains. Nevertheless, she believes the *Garbage Pail Kids* program injects a shot of irreverence into the Saturday morning cartoon line-up. It is designed to be different than cartoons such as *Care Bears*, and *Pound Puppies*.

Judy Price is known for her different programming. She is responsible for other CBS programs that have also directed harmful messages at kids. One of them, *My Dissident Mom*, encouraged children to get involved in the campaign to dismantle America's nuclear deterrent. Another, *What if I'm Gay?*, told students that homosexuality is a normal lifestyle and that they don't have to worry about catching AIDS if they take precautions and get certain information.

Prior to the scheduling of the *Garbage Pail Kids*, Price had been quoted as making a startling admission about the standards at CBS. She told one newspaper that when it comes to issues affecting teenagers, nothing was off limits for the network. The article said she got into children's programming for a surprising reason—she could get more controversial subject matter past the network censors than with adult programming. The article reported, "She said that she has found CBS extremely receptive to her ideas, despite societal pressure to keep programming for children noncontroversial." Well, the *Garbage Pail Kids* program is certainly controversial, and it may finally generate the backlash that puts her job in jeopardy.

September 18, 1987

144

The Media Campaign Against RENAMO

The media's misleading reporting on Mozambique

One of the most successful tactics the Communists have used against the Nicaraguan freedom fighters is to accuse them of horrible atrocities. This is now being used against the anti-communist guerrillas in Africa. They are known as the Mozambique Resistance, or RENAMO. The aim is to discredit them and weaken support for their cause. But the campaign against RENAMO may have gotten out of hand. The August 24th *Newsweek* went so far as to claim that RENAMO guerrillas have eaten children.

In a story about an alleged rebel reign of terror in Mozambique, reporter Ray Wilkinson claimed that a farmer from one village said that he saw the guerrillas kill and eat several children. Relief officials in the capital of the communist country are quoted as saying, in another case, the guerrillas cut the heart out of a woman and ate it in front of her surviving child.

Newsweek apparently wants its readers to believe these extraordinary accounts. They follow much-publicized stories in late July or early August of an alleged RENAMO attack on a village that left 400 dead. RENAMO was accused of shooting pregnant women and bayoneting new-born babies. These stories were based exclusively on information provided by the Marxist regime or its supporters.

While the media are quick to report the claims of the Marxist regime, they are less willing to obtain and publicize RENAMO's side of the story. RENAMO says the incident was actually government suppression of a mutiny by local militia against government forces. Many residents of the area were murdered, RENAMO says, in retaliation for the upris-

145

ing. The atrocity stories against RENAMO surfaced at a time when the Senate was preparing to take up the nomination of Melissa Wells as Ambassador to Mozambique. Wells was on record against recognizing or even talking to RENAMO. She had pledged to pursue the State Department policy of trying to accommodate the Marxist regime and somehow wean it away from the Soviet-bloc.

Republican Senators Jesse Helms of North Carolina and Bob Dole of Kansas led the opposition to her confirmation. Last July 14th, on the very day that Secretary of State George Shultz met with Helms and Dole in an effort to persuade them to back off Wells, *The Washington Post* and *The New York Times* published lead editorials viciously attacking RENAMO and its supporters. Tom Schaaf of the Mozambique Information Office, which supports RENAMO, says that media bias against the guerrillas also is reflected in the failure of network news reporters to visit RENAMO-controlled areas of the country, even though they have been invited to do so. But Schaaf said that the Christian Broadcasting Network cable channel has done a story based on such a trip.

The media campaign against RENAMO suffered a setback when *The Washington Post* on August 23rd published a story by an American missionary who had supposedly been kidnapped by the guerrillas. She said she was apprehended and then released by the guerrillas because they feared that government troops would murder her and others in her group and then blame it on the resistance. She said she was well-treated during the time she was with the guerrillas.

September 15, 1987

146

CBS
Never
Apologizes

CIA and Nicaraguan freedom fighters are exonerated of charges of drug trafficking. How Dan Rather misreported. . . denied. . . "scandalous, defamatory reporting"

Information released by the Iran-arms affair committees on August 25 exonerated the CIA and the Nicaraguan freedom fighters of much-publicized charges they had engaged in drug trafficking. But the exoneration wasn't mentioned by any of the network evening news programs.

Not only did the CBS *Evening News* not report the vindication of the CIA and the freedom fighters, but Dan Rather twisted the information released by the committees in such a way as to suggest that the CIA had been lying about the matter all along. It's no wonder that CIA-haters like Amy Carter exist. She must watch Dan Rather.

Rather reported, "Testimony from the CIA Task Force Chief for Central America alleges that one of the original Contra groups was involved in drug trafficking. The testimony is from Alan Fiers. He testified privately before the Iran-Contra investigating committees. Part of his testimony made public today says the CIA had considerable evidence linking the Nicaraguan rebel group headed by Eden Pastora to cocaine trafficking. This is one reason, Fiers said, that the United States broke ties with Pastora's group. Pastora and the CIA have repeatedly denied such talk, calling it a smear."

Rather thus left the impression that a CIA witness had now confirmed what the CIA had previously denied. This is false and CBS knows it.

The agency had been denying charges that it had condoned alleged drug smuggling by the freedom fighters. These

147

charges had been prominently reported on the CBS *Evening News* with Dan Rather and the CBS News program *West 57th*. The agency had referred to one of these broadcasts as "scandalous defamatory journalism at its worst." Contrary to what Dan Rather implied, the CIA had not said that talk of a drug link to Pastora's group was a "smear." In fact, the Reagan Administration itself admitted in a report submitted to Congress in 1986 that some members of the Pastora group may have been involved in drug smuggling. The contents of this report were publicized at the time by the Associated Press. The Fiers testimony released by the Iran-arms Committees was consistent with what the Administration and the CIA had been saying.

Dan Rather should have reported that the U. S. broke ties with the Pastora group after the drug connection surfaced, confirming the CIA position that it did not engage in or condone drug trafficking. The testimony exonerated the CIA of the charges that had been made by CBS News!

Rather completely ignored the contents of a congressional memorandum made public with the Fiers testimony that also confirmed the CIA position. Written by Robert A. Bermingham, an investigator for the House panel, it states, "There was no information developed indicating any U.S. Government agency or organization condoned drug trafficking by the Contras or anyone else." This memo, summarizing a massive investigation that included hundreds of interviews, also stated, "Despite numerous newspaper accounts to the contrary, no evidence was developed indicating that Contra leadership or Contra organizations were actually involved in drug trafficking."

September 11, 1987

148

CBS
Sinks
Even Lower

CBS coverage of 4th anniversary of KAL Flight 007 disaster

CBS reached a new low when it observed the fourth anniversary of the Soviet massacre of the 269 passengers and crew on Korean Air Lines flight 007 by airing two broadcasts promoting the Soviet line that the civilian airliner overflew Soviet territory because it was on a spy mission. This was the second time in six months that CBS had served Soviet interests by broadcasting a major Soviet disinformation theme. Last March, Dan Rather, on the CBS *Evening News*, reported as news, a Soviet claim that the AIDS virus had been created in a U. S. Army biological warfare laboratory. CBS had steadfastly refused to tell its viewers that this is a lie the Soviets have been peddling for nearly two years.

The anniversary of the shooting down of KAL 007 by the Soviets, which fell on September 1, should have been an occasion to remind Americans of the disdain that the communists showed for human life and civilized conduct just four years ago. But CBS didn't do that. Nor did it point out that the Kremlin, even under the supposedly more enlightened rule of Mikhail "Glasnost" Gorbachev, has never acknowledged that it was wrong to have shot down the airliner nor offered any apology, much less compensation, to the families of the victims.

Quite the contrary. CBS marked this tragic anniversary by devoting two segments of its *Morning Show*, on August 28 and August 31, to interviews with the author of a book who lends support to the Soviet disinformation theme that the Korean airliner was deliberately invading Soviet airspace on an intelligence mission. This is the line that the Soviets have taken from the beginning to justify their barbaric deed. Only four short years later, we find CBS telling its viewers, in effect, that the U. S. government has lied and deceived them and that the Soviets were telling the truth all along.

The author is a young man named David Pearson, who achieved considerable notoriety three years ago. Then a graduate student in sociology, Pearson published an article in the left-wing *Nation* magazine that supported the Soviet claim that KAL 007 was on a spy mission. His article was promptly demonstrated to be riddled with serious factual errors that totally undermined its credibility.

For example, there is a recording of the conversations that the pilot of the Soviet interceptor that shot down the airliner had with the ground. The International Civil Aviation Organization (ICAO), which investigated the affair, translated the pilot's statement as: "Roger. Target is flying with strobe light, with strobe light." Eight minutes later, the pilot said: "The air navigation lights are burning. The strobe light is on."

If anything is fatal to the spy plane theory it is evidence that the airliner was knowingly flying this dangerous mission over Soviet territory with its navigation lights on and its strobe light blinking. Pearson disposed of that inconvenient evidence very simply. He construed the pilot to be saying that his own lights were on and that he was blinking them as a signal to the airliner.

Pearson is simply not taken seriously by responsible analysts of the KAL 007 affair because of his cavalier disregard of the facts. Seymour Hersh, prominent journalist and author who is well known for his leftist views, disappointed the left last year when he published a book on KAL 007 in which he acknowledged that the spy mission story would not hold water. Both the House and Senate Intelligence Committees found Pearson's charges baseless. The House committee said its inquiry showed that "U. S. intelligence did not promote or even passively subscribe to an overlight and the Soviet attack."

The *CBS Morning Show* co-host, Rolland Smith, seemed oblivious to the cloud that was hanging over his guest, David

150

Pearson. He introduced him saying, "This morning we're going to talk about what really happened (in the KAL 007 case)." No one was on the program on either day to dispute Pearson's charges, and CBS has so far turned a deaf ear to demands that it air a rebuttal. They are proving how much the fairness doctrine is needed.

September 4, 1987

The Miami Herald's Smear Of Colonel North

Says North planned to suspend Constitution

Lt. Col. Oliver North was accused of many things. But the most sensational was helping draw up a controversial plan to suspend the U. S. Constitution in the event of a national crisis. This allegation was publicized in a front page story by *The Miami Herald*. Senator David Boren, Democrat of Oklahoma, asked North about the report during the Congressional Iran-arms hearings. North categorically denied it. That denial was reported back on page 11 by *The Miami Herald*.

The Herald story of a North plan to suspend the Constitution wasn't news only in Miami. Senator Boren said the article had caused "great concern" among the American people. He noted that the allegation had been carried "in several other newspapers" and by the wire services. "And I admit," Boren added, "it caused grave concern to me when I read these reports."

But North was asked by Boren to respond to an allegation that hadn't been attributed to anyone or anything. The story by Alfonso Chardy of *The Miami Herald* Washington bureau simply reported as fact that North "helped draw up a controversial plan to suspend the Constitution in the event of a national crisis, such as nuclear war, violent and widespread internal dissent or national opposition to a U. S. military invasion abroad." It is amazing that a detailed but baseless charge such as this should have been given national media attention. The finger should have been pointed not at North but at *The Miami Herald*. The newspaper should have been asked to back up its allegation.

Senator Boren read the above statement from the article and asked North if it were true. "Absolutely not," he replied.

152

Boren wanted to know if North was aware of any such plan. "No, sir. None," he said. In reporting North's denial back on page 11, the Herald implied that North may not have been telling the whole truth. It claimed that North had worked closely with the Federal Emergency Management Agency (FEMA) from 1982 to 1984 on national security matters. It said one official had claimed North was in FEMA headquarters two or three times a week during that period to discuss plans for dealing with nuclear war or insurrection. Notice that the allegation that North had helped draw up the plan to suspend the Constitution had been changed to the claim that he just participated in discussions on various plans. Maybe the Herald wasn't telling the full truth.

FEMA's alleged involvement in formulating such plans was the subject of two columns by Jack Anderson back in 1984. In fact, Anderson charged that one of FEMA's plans was to suspend the Constitution in the event of a national emergency. Anderson did not, however, try to implicate North in the preparation of this plan. He did not even mention the name of North. There was another important distinction between the versions of Anderson and *The Miami Herald.* The Herald said the plan was just one aspect of a "secret government" outside the traditional executive departments. Anderson said the plan was simply a draft proposal for standby legislation that would have to be approved by Congress if an emergency was at hand.

The Miami Herald said in an editorial that its story had provided evidence of a secret conspiracy that it found "chilling." But the only chilling feature of this case is the Herald's willingness to publicize something the evidence says is not true.

August 27, 1987

Can
Newsweek
Be Trusted?

Newsweek says Cardinal may have received funds from CIA

Newsweek magazine recently ran a story claiming that Oliver North was a source for a story it ran about the Achille Lauro terrorist incident several years ago. *Newsweek's* claim, if true, is a violation of journalistic rules against disclosing sources. The magazine's behavior is regarded as unprofessional by other newsmen. But *Newsweek* has also broken faith with its readers by publishing rumors and allegations.

At issue is a June 15th article about alleged secret U. S. aid to the Nicaraguan Catholic Church. The article claimed that the church of Cardinal Obando y Bravo may have received funds from the CIA and Oliver North's private network. Henry Ferror of Concerned Catholics for Religious Freedom in Nicaragua spoke for many when his letter to the editor appeared in a later issue. He said, "Publishing this piece, given the religious persecution taking place in Nicaragua, shows an incredible lack of judgment. (*Newsweek* presented) no evidence to support the claim that Cardinal Miguel Obando y Bravo received money from Lt. Col. Oliver North and the CIA. You simply state that some of the contributions Obando received 'may have' come from them."

In response to that letter, *Newsweek* said it stands by the story. *Newsweek* said it was based on highly knowledgeable sources in the U.S. and Central America. But the obvious question is, how could these sources be truly knowledgeable when they spoke in terms of what may have been, rather than what actually happened?

We had protested this story in a letter to Katharine Graham, Chairman of the Washington Post Company, which owns *Newsweek*. Robert Rivard, chief of correspondents of *Newsweek*, responded on her behalf. He also defended the story. In fact, he said the magazine may have reported the story with more caution than was necessary. But he failed to come up with any evidence to support *Newsweek's* charges.

He tried to turn the tables on us by claiming that he had found no evidence to support our charges. Our charges were simply that the story was based on speculation and hearsay, and that it had placed the life of the Nicaraguan Cardinal in jeopardy. We stand by those charges. As long as *Newsweek* refuses to prove its allegations are true, they remain just speculation and hearsay. And the Cardinal's life has been placed in jeopardy because of the religious persecution in Nicaragua. The specific *Newsweek* allegations against his church were highly publicized by the government-controlled media. The Cardinal himself stated that the extraordinary attention given to the *Newsweek* story could signify a new Sandinista campaign against his church. There is simply no doubt that the Sandinistas would prefer the Cardinal to be gone from the scene.

Newsweek's sources have proven unreliable in the past. The March 2nd *Newsweek* carried a sensational cover story titled, *Cover-Up.* It claimed that staffers on the National Security Council had said White House Chief of Staff Don Regan ordered them to conceal certain aspects of the Administration's initiative to Iran. But the Tower Board report that was later released found no evidence of Regan's involvement in such a cover-up. No such evidence surfaced in the Iran-arms hearings, and Regan joked about the allegation having appeared in a "leading news magazine."

August 21, 1987

155

Mangling
The News
At ABC

Peter Jennings on ABC's "World News Tonight"
misinforms on Contra human rights violations

On July 29, Peter Jennings read the following report on ABC's *World News Tonight*: "The State Department said today it was satisfied with the new study citing human rights abuses by the Nicaraguan contras. The report by the Nicaraguan Association for Human Rights was paid for by the U. S. Congress. It found that the contras had executed Sandinista prisoners that they had captured and civilians, including the American, Benjamin Linder."

In that three-sentence report, Jennings managed to misinform his viewers two ways. First, he gave the impression that the human rights report was simply another condemnation of atrocities committed by the Nicaraguan freedom fighters. Second, he suggested by using the word "executed" that the report had confirmed the claims of the Sandinistas that Benjamin Linder had been killed by a shot to the head fired at point-blank range. The freedom fighters say that Linder, an American leftist who went to Nicaragua to help the Sandinistas, was killed in a firefight.

The fifty-one page report covered investigations of 22 cases of human rights abuses by the freedom fighters, but it said that the investigators had discovered 200 allegations of abuses by the Sandinistas. Seventy specific instances of Sandinista abuses are detailed in the report. ABC News said nothing whatever about that, but neither did the Associated Press story on which it based its report. The misleading AP story was used by others, including *The Washington Post*.

Fortunately, *The Washington Times* took a look at the human rights report itself instead of simply relying on the AP, as ABC News did. The Times reported that the freedom fighters had cooperated with the investigators, giving them access to 72 Sandinista prisoners captured in recent months. A State Department spokesman was quoted as saying that the freedom fighters were the only resistance group that had offered such cooperation and which permitted a human rights watchdog group to monitor its activities. The spokesman said the freedom fighters were expected to take the charges seriously and to punish and expel those found guilty of abuses.

The ABC statement that the freedom fighters had "executed" Benjamin Linder could not be blamed on the Associated Press. The AP said the human rights investigators had concluded that Linder "was killed in an ambush by contras who had heard that a Sandinista patrol with a Cuban and another foreigner was in the area." It added: "There was conflicting testimony from participants as to whether Linder fired a weapon in battle. Because the Nicaraguan government refused to cooperate, the investigators could not corroborate a government coroner's report that Linder was shot point blank."

The Sandinistas and their leftist friends in this country got a lot of attention with their claim that Linder had been shot point blank, indicating deliberate execution. ABC, by using the word execution to describe Linder's death suggested that the investigators had confirmed this charge. This was obviously untrue. We promptly called this error to the attention of ABC News. Bill Lord, the executive producer of *"World News Tonight"*, didn't dispute it, but ABC has failed to follow its rules requiring prompt correction of errors. No correction has been aired.

August 19, 1987

157

Dan Rather Misfires In Afghanistan

Dan Rather claims U.S. "escalated the war"

For most of the eight years since the Soviet invasion of Afghanistan, the freedom fighters have been virtually defenseless against the Soviet airforce, including the deadly helicopter gunships. But during the last ten months the resistance has received and used effectively hundreds of anti-aircraft missiles, primarily the U. S. Stinger missile. Diplomats have estimated the resistance is shooting down an average of one Soviet aircraft a day using the missiles. An honest observer might say that the anti-aircraft missiles were a necessary and proper response to overwhelming Soviet airpower. But Dan Rather, in a recent CBS report documentary on Afghanistan, referred to the provision of these defensive weapons as a case of the United States having "escalated the war" in Afghanistan.

The documentary was titled, *"The Battle for Afghanistan"*. It featured extraordinary camerawork by Mike Hoover, including night photography of clashes between the Soviet army and the freedom fighters. But the script was seriously deficient. For example, Dan Rather said, "No one knows exactly why the Soviets invaded Afghanistan in 1979. No cameras were there at the time." Nevertheless, Rather tried to offer an explanation. He said the Soviets invaded because they wanted to create a buffer state between them and Islamic fundamentalism in Iran. The implication was that the Soviet invasion was a defensive move, designed to protect Soviet borders.

Experts in and out of the U.S. Government believe otherwise. They believe the Soviet invasion of Afghanistan was an offensive move designed to put them closer to the Persian

Gulf oil fields, the lifeline of many Western democracies. The 1984 edition of the Pentagon booklet, *Soviet Military Power*, says the invasion has enabled the Soviets to establish military bases "within striking distance" of those oil fields. At a time when U.S. policy in the Persian Gulf is a subject of strong debate, it would have been natural for Dan Rather and CBS News to have mentioned the Soviet military threat to the Gulf in Afghanistan. Instead, they completely ignored it.

Rather opened the broadcast by claiming that CBS News, since the invasion, has "received" 245 stories from inside Afghanistan. That sounds like a lot. But he didn't say how long these stories were, and how many of them actually were broadcast. Even if they all made it on the air, that averages only about 30 stories on Afghanistan a year, not even three a month. In the face of this lack of coverage, Rather had the gall to claim that the cause of the Afghans "has not captured the American imagination." He then suggested that his documentary may be the last serious look at the war for some time because journalists are supposedly finding it more difficult to get into the country.

On the positive side, the documentary did examine the terror tactics the Soviets are using. Rather said Soviet behavior in this war "makes even its friends uncomfortable." There was discussion of the small explosives and booby traps disguised as toys that the Soviets drop throughout the country to kill children, so there won't be a next generation to fight against them.

Again, however, these terror tactics weren't placed in the proper context. CBS News should have noted that experts believe the battle for Afghanistan is just one aspect of a much larger war for control of the Middle East and the Persian Gulf.

August 13, 1987

They Want
To Destroy
The President

*Washington Post runs front page story claiming President
"actively led initial effort to conceal his initiative to Iran"*

White House spokesman Marlin Fitzwater charged on
July 27 that "some members of the press are so hungry to
destroy the president that they've lost all perspective." His
comments, directed at *The Washington Post*, were front page
news in the Post and other newspapers. Of the evening news
programs, only ABC's *World News Tonight* reported Fitzwater's strong statement. ABC News White House correspondent Sam Donaldson dismissed it by saying that Fitzwater
was under "strain."

Fitzwater had reason to be agitated. The Post on July 26
had published a front page story by Walter Pincus and Dan
Morgan claiming that "newly released notes" of a November
10 White House meeting demonstrated that President Reagan
"actively led the initial effort last November to conceal the
essential details" of his initiative to Iran. These "notes"
were a major story on the evening news that Sunday night.
CBS News White House reporter Bill Plante said they showed
that, "at the very least, Mr. Reagan dissembled." This is a
polite way of calling the president a liar.

The truth was that these notes had been thoroughly examined by the Tower Board, whose report was released back on
February 26. The report said the notes, taken by Dr. Alton
Keel, acting deputy at the National Security Council, revealed
that "The President felt that a basic statement had to come
out but that we needed to avoid details and specifics of the
operation; he urged that we could not engage in speculation
because the lives of the hostages and the Iranians were at
stake."

160

Referring to these notes, the report said, "The Board found evidence that immediately following the public disclosure, the President wanted to avoid providing too much specificity or detail out of concern for the hostages still held in Lebanon and those Iranians who had supported the initiative. In doing so, he did not, we believe, intend to mislead the American public or coverup unlawful conduct." But the Post's July 26 front page story made it appear as though this was a brand new revelation in the Iran-Contra affair. The story included absolutely no reference to the Tower Board's explanation of the notes.

In making his complaint that "some members of the press" were out to "destroy" President Reagan over the Iran-Contra affair, spokesman Fitzwater said the president himself was "disturbed that this issue was so clearly reviewed by the Tower Board and so openly discussed at the time and somehow the facts have been overlooked in this case." The president appears to have a legitimate gripe, but the Post will never admit it. After all, this is the newspaper whose executive editor had been quoted as saying about coverage of the Iran-Contra affair, "This is the most fun we've had since Watergate." Walter Pincus, the Post reporter who helped resurrect the story about Keel's notes, has said he enjoys covering the affair because "all reporters want to have impact" and "all reporters want to take down the government . . ."

The resurrection of the story came at a time when the congressional hearings on the affair were drawing to a close. The hearings had produced no "smoking gun" linking the president to knowledge of the diversion of funds from the Iran arms sales to the Nicaraguan freedom fighters. The Post, eager to produce another Watergate and bring down another government, was desperate.

August 12, 1987

161

The New York Times Makes Another Error

Admits a Times story "went beyond Col. North's actual words and stated incorrectly . . ."

The New York Times published a very unusual front page correction on July 13th. A headline over an article referred to a correction of a previous article. Fox Butterfield acknowledged that a Times story about the testimony of Colonel Oliver North "went beyond Col. North's actual words and stated incorrectly that he had stated that neither the President nor Congress were to be informed" about a secret fund authorized by CIA director William Casey to underwrite activities. "In fact," Butterfield said, "the colonel has given no testimony so far that Mr. Casey intended to keep the existence of the fund secret from the President."

The writing of this story must have been very difficult for Fox Butterfield, since he had written that previous incorrect story. But this is just one of several embarrassments suffered by *The New York Times* in its coverage of the Iran arms story. Last December the Times published a page one story largely based on a report in the *Lowell Sun* that Oliver North knew of a scheme to divert $5 million in Iran arms profits into congressional campaigns. The Times admitted the next day that it couldn't confirm the story, which had been carried by newspapers around the country that use the Times news service.

The Times on February 15th published a front page story claiming that Oliver North's "Project Democracy" operations were the secret side of the National Endowment for Democracy, a federally funded group that provides money to Democratic organizations abroad. The story was false. But it was exploited by leftist and communist groups to discredit

162

organizations abroad that received assistance from the National Endowment for Democracy.

The Times published on June 1st a page one story that identified the real name of the CIA official who had secretly testified before the Iran-Nicaraguan hearings. This was after the White House had requested that news organizations not use his real name because the Intelligence Identities Protection Act of 1982 made it a federal crime to do so. The Washington bureau chief of the Times, Craig Whitney, professed ignorance of the White House request when we asked him about it. He insisted, however, that the Times had not violated the law. This claim will not be tested in court because White House spokesman Marlin Fitzwater ruled out any prosecutions of news organizations.

The Times published on June 18 a front page story that cited congressioal investigators on the Iran committees as the source for the charge that testimony would financially tie General Richard Secord to Edwin Wilson, the former CIA agent turned arms dealer to Libya. But the testimony never materialized, and the Secord-Wilson link was never proven.

August 4, 1987

CBS Smears Members Of Nicaragua Aid Network

CIA calls program scandalous, defamatory journalism at its worst

Colonel Oliver North's testimony was interrupted one day by two demonstrators who screamed statements about the Nicaraguan resistance fighters and drugs. These screams were treated as legitimate news on July 11th when the CBS News program "West 57th" attempted to implicate members of North's private aid network in narcotics trafficking.

This same program last April aired similar charges about the CIA's alleged involvement in drugs. The CIA called the program scandalous, defamatory journalism at its worst. Reporter Jane Wallace referred to this criticism when she introduced what turned out to be yet another episode of scandalous defamatory journalism. This time she tried to smear those Americans who had assisted Colonel North in getting much-needed help to the Nicaraguan freedom fighters.

Wallace said that Robert Owen, who served as the Colonel's liaison to the freedom fighters, may have been involved in a company that smuggled drugs. The program didn't mention that Owen was recently granted immunity by special prosecutor Lawrence Walsh. Owen would not have been granted immunity from prosecution if there had been any evidence linking him to illegal activities involving drugs.

The CBS program's attack on Owen troubled Senator Orrin Hatch, who asked North about it during his testimony. He said, "Rob Owen is the last person, besides me, that would ever be engaged in those kinds of activities. And when Mr. Owen found any information pertaining to the possibility of involvement in drugs, he told me, and I would tell the appropriate authorities. And there were several of such instances." North said the CBS report was "absolutely false."

Col. North went on to say that "We found no evidence during my tenure at the National Security Council that any of the resistance leaders were themselves or their supporters involved in drug running." In only one case, he said, was there some information about the possibility of drug smuggling, and that didn't involve any of the main resistance organizations. North's testimony on this issue wasn't mentioned by CBS News.

Based on the testimony of convicted drug dealers, the CBS program also tried to implicate Felix Rodriguez and John Hull in drug running and the private aid network. Rodriguez is a Bay of Pigs veteran, a former CIA operative, who assisted the private aid network in El Salvador. He has an honest reputation and he appeared before the Iran committees without an attorney present. Associates say that it is inconceivable that he would be involved in any way with drug trafficking. John Hull is an American rancher in Costa Rica who supports the freedom fighters. Jonathan Kwitny of *The Wall Street Journal* has admitted that Hull has provided details showing that drug planes could not have used his landing strips, as CBS and others have claimed.

The CBS charges are similar to those contained in a Chrtistic Institute law suit against the Nicaraguan freedom fighters and their supporters. They are viewed as an attempt to discredit members of the private aid network and divert attention away from the Sandinista drug connection.

August 3, 1987

NBC Does
A Number
On Bork

How Tom Brokaw and Chris Wallace manipulated
coverage to hurt Bork after his appointment

President Reagan's naming of Judge Robert Bork as an
associate Supreme Court justice severely tested the media's
commitment to fairness and objectivity. In a successful effort
to persuade President Reagan to veto the Fairness in Broadcasting Act, Walter Cronkite wrote to the president saying,
"We seek to govern ourselves by a standard of journalistic
ethics which requires us to present both sides of controversial
issues." Let's see how one network, NBC, carried out that
commitment in its reporting on the Bork appointment.

Tom Brokaw started off on the NBC *Nightly News* introducing Bork as "a highly regarded conservative judge probably best known for his role in firing Archibald Cox in the
Saturday night massacre during Watergate. He fired Cox after
Attorney General Elliot Richardson and his deputy William
Ruckelshaus refused President Nixon's order." Nowhere in
the broadcast did NBC point out that Richardson has praised
Bork's handling of this matter, saying that he himself had
urged Bork to stay on the job and carry out Nixon's order.

NBC's White House correspondent, Chris Wallace
showed a bit of Reagan's announcement of Bork's appointment. This was followed by civil rights activist Ralph Neas
charging that Bork would turn back the clock on civil rights.
Then came abortion rights activist Kate Michelman charging
that Bork's appointment would seriously endanger the right of
women to legal abortion. Next came Senator Howard Metzen-
baum of Ohio to declare that many senators were very upset
by the nomination.

Wallace then brought on Senator Edward Kennedy, saying Kennedy had "lashed out at Bork's role in the Saturday night massacre." Kennedy was shown saying, "The man who fired Archibald Cox does not deserve to sit on the Supreme Court of the United States." It would have been fair at this point, after hearing from four critics of Bork, to show Elliot Richardson setting the record straight on Bork's role in that event. That would have taken the edge off Senator Kennedy's attack, but NBC obviously did not want that.

But Chris Wallace was not oblivious to the need for balance. He introduced Senator Orrin Hatch, a Bork supporter, but he didn't show Hatch praising Bork or citing his qualifications for the job. Hatch was permitted to say only this: "I think you can play a little bit of politics for awhile, but I think that will wear very thin with the public at large."

Next NBC brought on its Justice Department reporter, Carl Stern, who described Bork as one who as a law professor had denounced government regulation of business and civil rights enforcement. Stern mentioned the Archibald Cox firing for the fourth time. He then listed a number of Bork's positions on issues, concluding with the statement that Bork believes "that there is no right of privacy." He neglected to say that what Bork argues is that nothing about a right of privacy is found in the Constitution. NBC finished up by putting on one more critic of Bork and a John Chancellor commentary proclaiming the Senate's right to refuse to confirm Bork on ideological grounds.

July 16, 1987

One-Sided News From South Africa

Two networks censor Botha's visit to Sharpeville and his good reception

For a year the news media have been complaining about South African censorship of news reports from that country. The press restrictions were designed to curb the reporting of violence that had become the staple diet of the media in 1986. From March 1 to June 5, 1986, 284 black South Africans had been killed by black radicals, 172 of them by being burned to death when tires filled with gasoline or diesel fuel were thrown around their necks and ignited. To halt this carnage, the South African government declared a state of emergency on June 12, 1986. It proceeded to detain several thousand blacks who were believed to be responsible for much of the violence and to restrict media coverage that it believed tended to encourage violent deeds.

These actions produced a dramatic change. There was a sharp decline in stories in our media from South Africa. The decline was even sharper with respect to stories involving violence. This reflected a genuine decline in terrorist activity. Black clergymen who visited this country not long after the state of emergency was declared said that they were now able to leave their churches unguarded and sleep peacefully in their homes. They said that had been impossible for many months, since they and their churches had been targets of the black radicals.

It was made clear that there had been a dramatic improvement in the situation when South Africa announced June 2, that the number of persons detained for more than a month under the state of emergency was down to 1,480.

This confirmed reports that large numbers of detainees

168

had been released in recent weeks, including all but eleven of the 280 detainees under the age of 16. The government evidently felt that the climate had improved sufficiently to permit a significant degree of relaxation.

This confidence was put to the test on June 4, when State President P. W. Botha and members of his cabinet made a visit to Sharpeville, the black township where 69 blacks were killed and 200 wounded in 1960, when police opened fire on a crowd that was protesting South Africa's pass laws. Much to the surprise of foreign reporters, Botha was given what Peter Younghusband, correspondent for *The Washington Times*, described as a "tumultuous welcome" by "hundreds of foot-stamping, cheering blacks." He was made a freeman of Sharpeville and five neighboring townships. Botha in turn "ceremoniously granted 'freedom' to six townships in the region" and said the time had come for blacks and whites to negotiate a shared future.

The mayor of the six townships, Esau Mahlatsi, praised Botha as a great leader, and the two men clasped each other's hands and held them high over their heads to acknowledge the cheers of the crowd as the state president departed. Three years ago Mayor Mahlatsi and several of his councilmen had been forced to flee for their lives when they were attacked by black radicals. Four councilmen had been killed.

One would think that this was a story that our media could not ignore, but two of the three commercial networks did just that. CBS and NBC proved that censorship by the South African government is not the only impediment to the flow of news from that country. Self-censorship may be an even bigger impediment.

ABC News covered the Botha visit to Sharpeville, but it demonstrated its feelings about the story in correspondent Jim Hickey's lead. He said, "It was Botha's first visit to a black township in eight years, and critics condemned this trip as cynical and arrogant, for it was here in Sebokeng and in nearby Sharpeville that more than 60 people were killed in violent rent protests nearly three years ago." Hickey was off by 24 years. He went on to say that the visit "was carefully orchestrated," but as the camera focused on a sea of smiling, cheering blacks, he had to acknowledge that the reception was "enthusiastic." Hickey commented that this was "unusual and puzzling because black crowds normally protest the government, not cheer it."

The New York Times led its story with the statement that Botha had been "mobbed by hundreds of cheering blacks." *The Washington Post* started with "cheering and chanting" black children. ABC's Hickey did his best to undercut what his camera was showing.

June 12, 1987

How The
Media Disarm
America

*"West 57th" scares viewers about U.S. Government
research in biological warfare weapons . . . and avoids
looking at Soviet build-up*

One of the tactics used by the media to inhibit the build-up of America's national defense is to suggest the Soviet threat is non-existent and that we are provoking the military arms race. This tactic was used effectively on the May 26th edition of the CBS program *West 57th* in a story about biological warfare.

Correspondent John Ferrugia attempted to scare his viewers with various claims about U. S. Government research in the field. He said the research under the Reagan Administration had mushroomed more than 500 percent, and that this was only the beginning. He said world renowned scientists had warned that a proposed Pentagon laboratory on biological warfare could result in the release of the deadliest diseases on earth which could destroy entire populations. Ferrugia said these scientists and prominent public health officials had come to the conclusion that there is no biological warfare threat to the U. S. and that the proposed lab was offensive in nature.

Reporter John Ferrugia carefully avoided any serious look at Soviet biological warfare activities. There were only two vague references to that effort. Early in the program, Ferrugia said, "The Pentagon says it's studying these agents only for defensive purposes." Later, an Army official was permitted to say, "We believe some of these agents constitute a biological warfare threat, as well as natural disease threat." Ferrugia dismissed that, saying, "That's the Army's standard answer."

The facts show that the Reagan Administration's research in biological warfare is a response to alleged violations by the Soviets of the 1972 Biological Weapons Convention. A 1980 report of a Democratic-controlled subcommittee of the House Intelligence Committee concluded that the Soviets had deceived the U. S. about the outbreak of the deadly disease anthrax in the Soviet Union in 1979. The Soviets claimed that the disease, which killed 1,000 persons, came from tainted meat. But the subcommittee said the evidence showed it was linked to an explosion at a military facility long suspected of housing biological warfare activities.

Congressman Bill Young of Florida, a member of the subcommittee, said at the time, "The fact that the Soviets lied to the U. S. Government about the source of the epidemic indicates that again the Soviets are cheating after signing an agreement . . . Treaties and agreements with the Soviet Union should not be signed unless they are self-enforcing or if we have the capability to fully monitor them through our intelligence agencies or with on-site inspection."

If CBS had taken account of this information, it could have produced a story about how the U. S. Government is completely justified in its research into biological warfare in order to defend against the Soviets. Instead, CBS failed to tell the full truth about the massive Soviet effort in this field. Reporter John Ferrugia made a hero out of a character by the name of Jeremy Rifkin who has sued to stop the Army from constructing a biological warfare laboratory to develop the equipment necessary to protect our people and soldiers in the event of war. Rifkin was identified as the head of a group called the Foundation on Economic Trends. In fact, he has a background in the far left. He was once the leader of a group that expressed admiration for Lenin, Mao and Che Guevara.

June 11, 1987

172

State Department
Rebuts CBS
Drug Allegations

CBS News charges CIA has employed known drug smugglers to fly weapons to Nicaragua freedom fighters

CBS News has charged that the CIA has employed known drug smugglers to fly weapons to the Nicaraguan freedom fighters, and that on their return trips they have flown drugs to the United States to be sold to raise money for more weapons. These allegations have been featured on the CBS *Evening News* with Dan Rather, and the magazine-type program *West 57th*. The CIA has dismissed the charges as malicious and slanderous. Now the State Department has denied them.

The denial came during a congressional subcommittee hearing chaired by Democratic Congressman David Obey of Wisconsin. Obey asked Assistant Secretary of State Elliott Abrams what effort the department was making to investigate the CBS allegations. Abrams said the State Department asks the Drug Enforcement Administration to check the backgrounds of those involved in helping the resistance to make sure they are clean. He pointed out that the CBS allegations came from three convicted felons in prison on drug trafficking charges. Abrams cast doubt on the charges by noting that one of the felons had claimed that he was permitted to land a plane at Homestead Air Force Base in Florida loaded with 25,000 pounds of marijuana. He said this and other charges were not credible.

Ken Boehm of the organization Citizens for Reagan has also questioned the CBS charges. In a protest letter to CBS, Boehm noted that CBS sought to add credence to its unsubstantiated claims by alleging that the convicted drug dealers had little to gain from talking as they did. Boehm points out that *Newsweek* revealed last January that, on the contrary,

173

two of them were facing the prospect of long jail terms and were hoping to sell their story to prosecutors in exchange for immunity. Ken Boehm complained that the airing of the drug charges reflected a kind of journalism shabby even by the very low standards of CBS.

The May 4th issue of *U. S. News and World Report* looked into the allegations. It noted that Senator John Kerry, an opponent of the Nicaraguan freedom fighters, has investigated the charges but has failed to disclose any hard evidence. On the other hand, *U. S. News and World Report* found a lot of hard evidence of a Sandinista drug connection. It reported that the Sandinistas had eagerly established their own transshipment routes for Colombian cocaine because they were pressed for hard currency and wanted a share of profits from the dope trade. *U. S. News* reported that the Sandinistas had even opened their own refineries for drugs.

U. S. News quoted a former Sandinista diplomat as saying that Nicaragua became involved in drugs at the direction of Castro's Cuba. He said drug trafficking produced "a very good economic benefit which we needed for our revolution. We wanted to provide food to our people with the suffering and death of the youth of the United States."

Rather than report that kind of information, CBS News airs unsubstantiated charges that smear the Nicaraguan freedom fighters and the U. S. agency, the CIA, that supports them. It's no wonder that Ken Boehm of Citizens for Reagan reports that complaints from his 100,000 members list CBS by name as the most biased source of news in this country.

May 19, 1987

PBS
Does It
Again

PBS program "War On Nicaragua" completely distorts facts . . . criticizes America . . .

The Reagan Administration has lied about Nicaragua, the Sandinistas want peace, American soldiers are corrupt and freedom fighters are terrorists. These were the messages presented by the taxpayer supported Public Broadcasting Service (PBS) in an April 21st program called "War on Nicaragua."

The program was narrated by William Greider, a national correspondent for *Rolling Stone*, a magazine that mainly covers rock and roll music. Greider, a former editor for *The Washington Post*, said in a 1981 article that the American defense build-up was criminally wasteful and that right-wing mystics had invented Red Ghosts in order to scare the public into spending more money on defense. Greider said the defense problem didn't exist and that we were responding to "nonexistent threats."

Despite those views, or perhaps because of them, Greider was selected to do a program on Nicaragua. Not surprisingly, he did not discover the Communist Sandinista regime in Nicaragua to be a threat to the United States or even to its neighbors. In fact, he reported that the Sandinistas had mounted a major diplomatic initiative to come to terms with Washington in 1983. Sandinista foreign minister Miguel D'Escoto told Greider that Secretary of State George Shultz was out on the golf course and didn't have time to consider their plan. Greider ignored the evidence that shows the Sandinistas have adamantly refused to negotiate with the democratic resistance, and have stalled on negotiations with the United States over the last several years.

Much of Greider's program was devoted to portraying the

175

Nicaraguan freedom fighters as terrorists. The program was preceded by a message that it contained graphic scenes of war and that viewer discretion was advised. Incredibly, not one leader of the resistance was interviewed by Greider. Former Reagan officials and military men were interviewed. But they were presented in a context of explaining why the U. S. had decided to conduct a war aimed at civilians against the sovereign government of Nicaragua. Supporters of the U. S. policy came across as paranoid killers.

There were several other major problems with Greider's show. He ignored evidence that the Sandinistas have continued to arm the Salvadoran guerrillas, and that they have lied about it. However, Greider did accuse the Administration of not telling the truth about its objectives in Nicaragua. The program also smeared U. S. servicemen in Central America. When a former military official was heard saying that Americans should establish friendly relationships with the people of Central America, the program showed film of G.I.'s on military training missions in Honduras. This was followed by film of off-duty G.I.'s carousing with local Honduran girls and a Honduran youth who flashes an obscene gesture. Finally, viewers were shown film of Honduran women dressed like prostitutes. The message was that our presence was corrupting the people.

Greider claimed that the Iran arms affair was a product of the Administration's policy of supporting the Nicaraguan freedom fighters. He called it an epic scandal linked to a proxy war. But he was wrong again. It was the lack of congressional support for the policy that prompted Lt. Colonel Oliver North and his associates to go to extraordinary lengths to help the resistance.

May 7, 1987

176

Media Ignore Communists At Demonstration

Media conceal Communist involvement in the April 25th Mobilization For Peace and Justice in Central America and South Africa

The April 25th Mobilization for Peace and Justice in Central America and South Africa was the lead item on the NBC *Nightly News* that night. A crowd estimated at 75,000 marched in Washington and about half that many marched in San Francisco. The closest that reporter Candy Crowley got to acknowledging a Communist role in the event was when she said there was "a cause for everyone and someone for every cause." At that point, if you had a sharp eye, you could have picked out a Communist Party banner in the demonstration. On ABC's *Evening News* program reporter Dennis Troute said the affair was organized by a group representing "trade unionists, women's groups, church and peace activists."

Their failure to report the Communist Party involvement is despicable because the role of the party and its supporters had become a major issue prior to the demonstration. A piece of literature distributed out of the Mobilization's national office listed the Communist Party as an endorser. One day before the march, Stephen Rosenfeld of *The Washington Post* said the party's role posed a major problem for those participating in the event.

Despite ABC reporter Dennis Troute's reference to trade unionists involved in the event, AFL-CIO chief Lane Kirkland had warned members of labor unions not to participate on the grounds that the organizers and speakers opposed democracy in Central America. Kirkland's warning had been reported in *The Washington Times* and in Rosenfeld's column

177

in the Post. Rosenfeld also acknowledged that the organizers included groups that "work easily with the Central America left, including the violent anti-democratic left."

In its news report on the demonstration, the Post ignored the Communist Party's role. Near the end of the story the Post acknowledged that Kirkland had "urged workers to avoid the protest," but didn't say why Kirkland had issued the warning. The Post and NBC and ABC ignored the revelation in *The Washington Times* that the organizers of the event had received $3 million from Nicaragua's Marxist regime. Reporter George Archibald quoted an ex-Sandinista military official with ties to the regime as saying that the money came out of a huge grant of military and economic aid given to the regime in March by Libya.

The charges by *The Washington Times* came just one day before the protest. They were picked up by the Associated Press wire service, which quoted organizers as saying they were laughable. The Times story was denounced by speakers at the rally, including actor Ed Asner, who said that the Times, the Reagan Administration and the Nicaraguan freedom fighters should all go to hell.

Although Stephen Rosenfeld of the Post said demonstrators would find it difficult to answer complaints about Communist Party involvement, the Newspaper Guild said through a spokesman that it did not care. It said the party's role was of no concern. This is the union that represents journalists at such newspapers as *The Washington Post*, and the news magazines and the wire services. The Guild, which is affiliated with the AFL-CIO, remained as a sponsor despite Lane Kirkland's warning.

May 6, 1987

The Other Face Of The Nicaraguan Resistance

"Doonesbury" cartoon strip degenerates into left-wing political diatribe on Nicaragua

The *Doonesbury* cartoon strip is found on the funny pages, but it's not very funny most of the time. Authored by Gary Trudeau, husband of NBC *Today Show* host Jane Pauley, it frequently degenerates into a left-wing political diatribe. On Sunday, April 12th, his target was the Nicaraguan resistance movement. It showed Assistant Secretary of State Elliott Abrams being grilled before a congressional committee over his support for the Nicaraguan freedom fighters. He was accused by Congress of supporting an "Army of thugs" and of spending his time trying to deodorize "the permanently smelly." After Abrams defends the freedom fighters, the scene shifts to Nicaragua, where two resistance fighters are shown having shot their way into a house. One fighter says, "I got one. I got a Communist." His partner says, "Maybe two. She looks pregnant."

Tomas Regalado, news director for a Miami radio station, tells a far different story about the Nicaraguan resistance and its leaders. He wrote a recent article based on a trip to the Nicaraguan frontier that describes what he calls "the other face" of those battling the Sandinistas. He says it's a story the Big Media have not found enough time to report.

Regalado's report focused on Enrique Bermudez, the military chief of the Nicaraguan Democratic Force, the largest group of resistance fighters. He says Bermudez spends a lot of his time performing a function that the U. S. media never report on—listening to the problems of civilians and soldiers. Regalado reported that a parade of such people visits with Bermudez. Each one goes in with a problem, and each one

179

leaves with a solution—either money or authorization for medicine, food or clothing.

Regalado says the American media have not shown the humanitarian clinic located near a resistance camp, where sick children are attended to every day. He says these sick children are given medicine made possible by the humanitarian aid given by the United States. He says the American reporters have also failed to visit the small warehouse, filled only with medicine for children. Nor have they found time to visit the dental clinic, where civilians and soldiers are given treatment.

Regalado says the media "have not been able, either, to visit one of the hospitals, as we did, very close to the Nicaraguan border, where the attention is not only for soldiers, but also for civilians, such as the old peasant who was brutally beaten by two Sandinistas (for crossing into Nicaraguan territory).

He says nothing is written in the big U. S. media about these things. Instead, the media spent their time trying to make sure that every penny of humanitarian aid is accounted for on some bank statement in Washington. "Unfortunately," Regalado says, "the big media do not know how to count, or where to look." The media prefer the *Doonesbury* caricature of the resistance forces. They like to portray the freedom fighters as terrorists and thugs. The American people must realize that there is another side of the story, another face that could be seen and verified if only the media would take the time.

April 28, 1987

No
Surge
Of Racism

How the media give impression of upsurge in racism by providing concentrated coverage of incidents

Some of our news media have been telling us that the country is engulfed with a dangerous new flood of racist feeling. *Time* magazine tells its readers that there has been an "upsurge" of racism. It says racism "like a poisonous weed has sprouted in various forms at campuses across the U. S." Lawrence Wade, a black columnist for *The Washington Times*, says this is a phony story. Indeed, he says it is the phoniest story since *Washington Post* reporter Janet Cooke made up a story about a non-existent 8-year-old heroin addict and won a Pulitzer Prize with it.

Years ago a journalist and author named Lincoln Steffens described how a newspaper can create a crime wave. All it has to do is start printing stories about all the crimes recorded on the police blotter each day. The public will get the impression that the community has been engulfed with crime when, in fact, the only thing that has happened is that the newspaper is *reporting* more crime. Lawrence Wade feels that something like this is going on now with respect to racist incidents.

There have been a handful of well publicized incidents. A gang of white youths attacking three young black men in the New York community, Howard Beach, attacks on black marchers in all-white Forsyth County, Georgia, and a prank at the South Carolina military school, the Citadel, where some white students donned sheets and mimicked the Ku Klux Klan, are the most highly publicized cases. There was also a disturbance on the campus of the University of Massachusetts at Amherst involving white versus black students,

181

and a student radio station on the campus of the University of Michigan was shut down after it aired some racist jokes.

The far left, and especially the Communist Party, USA, eagerly seized on these isolated incidents to bolster their contention that minority groups in this country are persecuted and discriminated against. Angela Davis, a black professor who co-chairs the Communist Party's National Alliance Against Racist and Political Repression, has been comparing these incidents to what used to happen in the Deep South before the civil rights reforms of the 1960s.

It's easy for the media to play up a few incidents and conclude that they are proof of a nationwide trend, but Lawrence Wade says they ought to take a look at the statistical evidence, such as it is. He points out that in 1986 there were 35 percent fewer complaints of discrimination because of race or national origin filed with the Department of Education than in 1980. He says that the Department of Housing and Urban Development statistics show a 10 percent decline in discrimination complaints involving housing from 1982 to 1986.

The Equal Employment Opportunity Commission reports a 30 percent increase in complaints of racial discrimination in employment during the Reagan years, but Wade notes that the biggest surge was from 1979 to 1980, when such complaints jumped 90 percent. That was during the Carter administration. There are plenty of cases of white attacks on black and black attacks on white to feed media-generated "upsurge of racism" if that's the way our media choose to play it. That's the way Angela Davis and her comrades in the Communist Party would like them to play it. Let's hope they show better judgment.

April 24, 1987

CBS
Battles
CIA

CIA says CBS program "West 57th" airs false attack just to generate ratings and profits

Would a television network air a false attack on the CIA just to generate ratings and profits? That's what the CIA says. The agency has released a hard hitting statement attacking CBS program, *West 57th*, for a story on April 6, 1987, that tried to link the CIA to drug smugglers. The CIA condemned the program as "scandalous defamatory journalism at its worst." It said CBS had reason to know the information it put on the air was false, and that the report was mud-slinging designed to improve the program's chances of staying on the air. "It is outrageous," the CIA says, "for CBS to inflict such totally false and misleading information on the viewing public."

There is no question that a lot was riding on this particular program. It marked the first time in eight months that an episode of *West 57th* had aired. If it didn't achieve good ratings, it might be cancelled. The CBS *Evening News* with Dan Rather hyped it by including a special story promoting the program. He introduced reporter Jane Wallace, whose story was to feature the drug charges against the CIA. After showing her interview with one of the CIA's accusers, Dan Rather told his viewers that there was a lot more to the story and they should tune into *West 57th* if they wanted the rest of it.

Wallace's story was the first on the program that night. She introduced it claiming that CBS had uncovered "new and startling information that indicates the American government got involved in smuggling drugs to supply the Nicaraguan Contras." By government, she meant the CIA. She claimed the CIA employed known drug smugglers to fly weapons to the resistance forces, and that they would return with drugs that would be sold to raise money to buy more weapons.

Jane Wallace claimed that three dozen sources had confirmed this "basic scheme," but her report relied on only three—all of them convicted drug dealers. She justified her reliance on these sources by claiming that they had nothing to gain from making the charges. But it's important to remember that these charges are not new. *The New York Times* had a story about them last February. The Times quoted federal drug officials as saying the convicted drug traffickers behind the charges "are selling a story to Congress and to the media that they have concocted to have their sentences reduced or to have their cases dismissed." That statement carefully indicates that the drug dealers have a lot to gain.

The Washington Times reported that George Morales, one of Jane Wallace's sources, actually talked to the staff of Senator John Kerry about getting immunity from prosecution in return for his testimony before a Senate panel. Immunity wasn't granted, but Morales may still be hoping to get his sentence reduced in exchange for testimony. Senator Kerry has been leading congressional efforts to prove there is a link between government officials, drug traffickers and the Nicaraguan resistance. He is a strong critic of U. S. policy in Central America.

The Times said another of Wallace's sources, Michael Tolliver, has been described by federal officials as "a habitual liar" who was arrested 6 times on drug charges.

April 22, 1987

CNN
Defends The
Indefensible
Network reporter misleads America about Nicaragua

Ted Turner's *Cable News Network* advertises itself as the world's most important network, committed to the highest standards of journalistic integrity. That reputation has been in doubt since evidence surfaced showing that the network has been used to serve the interests of Turner's friends in the Kremlin. During the opening of the Goodwill athletic games he sponsored with the Soviet Union, his network suppressed news about the arrest of a prominent Soviet dissident. The network has adamantly refused to investigate why the information was suppressed and guarantee that it won't happen again.

Ted Turner is also an opponent of aid to the Nicaraguan freedom fighters, and his network was recently caught in the act of airing a dubious story designed to discredit those forces. When the flawed report was brought to the attention of CNN management, the response was that, despite evidence to the contrary, the report was accurate and fair. This controversy shows that CNN fails to uphold the minimal standards in journalism.

CNN aired, on March 31st, a report by its correspondent in Nicaragua, Lucia Newman, about what she called the "Contra war." This is an odd way of describing a war in which two sides, the resistance forces and the Sandinistas, are engaged. By referring to it as the "Contra war," Newman was suggesting it was the responsibility of just one side, the Contras or the freedom fighters. In fact, it can be argued that it is the "Sandinista War," since evidence shows that the resistance emerged only after the Sandinistas started a war against their neighbors and the Nicaraguan people.

185

But the worst part of her report included film footage and commentary of what were supposed to be victims of the resistance forces. Her report featured a 13-year old boy and 55-year old man on crutches. Newman said they each lost a leg when a "Contra road mine" exploded under a bus they were riding in. She said nine people, including two children died, and that at least a dozen others were injured.

Newman did not cite any evidence whatsoever that it was, in fact, a Contra road mine. She didn't say if she had seen the resistance forces planting it. She didn't report that she found a label on it that said it was the property of the resistance forces. It was not revealed just who or what was the source of this damaging allegation. To make matters worse, she didn't report a response from the target of the allegation. The Nicaraguan resistance forces weren't quoted as saying anything about this mine that they supposedly planted.

When these problems with the report were brought to the attention of CNN, we were told that network management had reviewed it and had concluded that it was "accurate and fair." But accuracy means verification, and there's not evidence her statement was checked or verified. The concept of fairness implies the other side was presented, but that was clearly not the case. It appears that reporter Newman was taken on a guided tour by the Communist Sandinistas and that she reported what they told her as fact. This is not journalism; it is propaganda or disinformation.

April 21, 1987

The Media
Go For
The Kill

TV network news stars report the "bad" and leave out the "good"

It was wall-to-wall people in the White House press briefing room as journalists stood in long lines waiting for release of the Tower Board report on the Iran arms affair. The magic moment came at 10 a.m. on February 26, 1987. It was a mad scramble to be first as the network news stars got their copies and went on the air to tell viewers what was in a report that they hadn't read or even opened.

A wire service reporter desperately thumbed through his copy as he ran to his typewriter in the nearby work area. A colleague told him, "Don't read it, just put it on the wire."

I was there. The mad rush itself became a story, as television cameras focused on journalists pushing and shoving and eventually grabbing up thousands of (free) copies.

One of the network stars, NBC News White House reporter Andrea Mitchell, didn't stand in line. She had someone do that for her. She remained positioned in front of a television camera, with microphone in hand, and quickly went "live" when an underling handed her a copy of the report. She told her viewers she hadn't read it, but already knew it was highly critical of various people.

Mitchell and her ilk were in a bind. They had less than an hour before the members of the Tower Board were to hold their news conference. "Help me," Mitchell pleaded, as she tried to pull out the most damaging material for later use. An assistant told her to look at section four, titled, "What Was Wrong."

Much of that section was critical of the president and his aides. But it also included the finding that the president "did not, we believe, intend to mislead the American public or cover-up unlawful conduct." The board said that . . . "the president took steps to ensure that all the facts would come out." It cited his request to Mr. Meese to look into the history of the initiative, his appointment of this board, his request for an Independent Counsel, his willingness to discuss this matter fully and to review his personal notes. The board said it was convinced that the president wants the full story to be told.

All three networks carried the commission's news conference live. They showed President Reagan opening up the news conference by saying that he was going to take several days to read the report and think about it. ABC News anchorman Peter Jennings interpreted this to mean that the president wasn't going to engage in "instant analysis," something that the networks specialize in. True to form, after the news conference ended, Jennings and his colleagues on ABC and the other networks immediately went to work to analyze what was in the 250 page report.

The evening news programs didn't highlight the positive statements about the president's role in the affair. They did note, however, that commission chairman Tower had stated that the president had made mistakes in his handling of the affair. What they didn't show was Tower's follow-up statement, "I might note that every president has made mistakes from time to time, some of far greater consequence than the ones that President Reagan has made." Tower described the Iran-Contra affair as an aberration in a successful administration.

March 11, 1987

188

Media Give
The FBI A
Black Eye

More biased reporting designed to turn Americans against the FBI

The media have given a lot of publicity to charges that the FBI wrongly investigated a group called the Committee in Solidarity with the People of El Salvador, CISPES. The charges were publicized on the front page of *The New York Times*, and on all three evening news programs. ABC News went so far as to name the individual making the charges, Margaret Ratner of the Center for Constitutional Rights, as its "Person of the Week".

"Person of the Week" is a designation reserved for those who have affected the news for better or worse. In this case, Jennings made it clear that ABC News held Ratner in high regard. He said that by making her charges public, "There's no doubt in our minds that what she and her colleagues accomplished is good for all Americans. It is an advertisment to the rest of the world that if an individual's rights are threatened here for any reason, there are always other individuals who will go to bat for them, using the legal system and the court of public opinion."

Nothing could be further from the truth. What ABC News and the other media have done is get duped into a propaganda campaign designed to undermine the FBI's ability to protect the American people from subversion and terrorism. The real truth behind this story shows just how easy it is for left-wing, even pro-Marxist groups to manipulate the news media.

Ratner and her colleagues wanted the public to believe there was no legitimate reason to investigate CISPES. The media cooperated by covering up the true nature of the organization. CISPES was portrayed by Ratner and the media as simply a group opposed to Reagan policies in Central America. In fact, its literature openly praises the Communist guerrillas in El Salvador. These guerrillas are fighting a democratically elected government. They have killed thousands of innocent people, including Americans. Captured guerrilla documents show that CISPES was formed by a representative of the guerrillas. The FBI had good reason to investigate under foreign counter-intelligence guidelines.

Ratner and her colleagues claim they obtained 1200 pages from FBI files relating to the investigation of CISPES. But at their well-attended news conference, they released only fifty of them. George Archibald of *The Washington Times* is apparently the only reporter who wondered what was in the rest of the pages. He discovered they included references to reports that CISPES was implicated in terrorism inside the United States. But this is nothing new. A former FBI informant in the group, who later turned against the FBI, testified last year that he received information that individuals posing as members of CISPES had threatened the life of President Reagan.

The media were quick to point out that no convictions resulted from the FBI investigation. The investigation was later closed. But that doesn't mean that the bureau doesn't have an obligation to investigate groups and individuals when it receives reports they are involved in possibly criminal activity. For the real story, the media should have taken a hard look at ABC's "Person of the Week," Margaret Ratner, and her group, the Center for Constitutional Rights. This was founded by Ratner's husband, the notorious far-left activist lawyer, William Kunstler. It has engaged in the defense of "violence-oriented prison inmates, terrorists and members of militant and Marxist-Leninist groups charged with serious crimes."

February 15, 1987

190

Why South Africa Expels American Reporters

Their reporting is so one-sided and inaccurate it is completely misleading the American public

South Africa has been portrayed by some of our politicians and some of our media as being the most repressive country in the world. This has astonished many Americans, including some reporters, who have visited that troubled land. They can't reconcile what they have seen with what the American reporters are saying. One of the things these visitors often discover is that all South African blacks are not followers of Archbishop Desmond Tutu, the one black South African who is regularly interviewed or quoted in the American media.

Black South Africans who disagree with Tutu's promotion of sanctions against South Africa have great difficulty getting their views known abroad. In the summer of 1986, a group of black clergymen came to this country to tell the American people that adoption of the sanctions bill then before our Congress would hurt South African blacks and that most blacks opposed that legislation. They were ignored by our Big Media. Asked if they had contact with American reporters in South Africa, one of them replied that our reporters there ignored them also.

The sanctions were imposed and now articles have begun to appear in some of our media reporting that blacks are indeed suffering from the disinvestment by American firms in South Africa. The evidence is growing that those who warned of the negative consequences of the sanctions legislation are being proved right. Those who depend on the media for information that will help them decide what position to take on issues such as this have a right to ask why they were not warned about this in advance.

The reason is clear. The American reporters in South Africa and their editors in this country were behaving as committed partisans in the push for sanctions. They viewed the denial of civil rights to blacks in South Africa as so evil that they were determined to help punish the "white minority government," as they always called it. That led them to play down the terrorism instigated by the communist-dominated African National Congress. When President Botha disclosed that in a three-month period, blacks had killed 284 blacks, 172 of them by lynching by fire, that went unreported by our media.

Our media also refused to report Botha's disclosure that the South African government had obtained a document outlining the plans for the South African Communist Party to promote the violent takeover of power, which would be followed by a massive redistribution of wealth, the liquidation of all opposition by revolutionary violence.

New York Times reporter Alan Cowell was one of those who ignored all this. Despite the wave of horrible lynchings and bombings, Cowell recently referred to "a threatened upsurge of what the Government calls terrorism." He said the authorities "assert they are the target of a revolutionary onslaught," suggesting this was a figment of their imagination. South Africa recently decided to expel Mr. Cowell and refused to admit a replacement. The Times claims this is because South Africa doesn't want the world to know the truth. The South Africans don't think Cowell was telling the truth about their country. They have a point, but more vigorous efforts to expose his bad reporting would have been a better response.

January 21, 1987

Public Television Whitewashes The Mandelas

Admitted terrorists misrepresented to American public

Nelson Mandela, the imprisoned leader of the African National Congress, is an admitted terrorist and pro-communist. His wife, Winnie, has endorsed the murder of moderate blacks by burning them alive. Yet the Mandelas came across in a recent public televison program as advocates of democracy in South Africa who believe in violence only as a last resort.

The program, *Mandela*, could have been produced by the African National Congress (ANC) and aired by Soviet television. Instead, the American taxpayers paid to have this aired in the United States via the Public Broadcasting Service (PBS). The program stands as further evidence of the corrupt programming practices at PBS.

It opened with a story about how Nelson Mandela's daughter had come to the realization that her daddy was in prison "because he was fighting for black people." The narrator declared that, "For seeking democratic rights for most of the people in South Africa, Nelson Mandela has been in jail since 1962." The daughter can't be faulted for having a sympathetic view of her father's plight. But the narrator, former ABC newsman Max Robinson, must be held accountable for his totally false statement. Mandela went to jail not for "seeking democratic rights," but for participating in a violent scheme to deny the rights of others.

Later in the program, Robinson provided a few more details about what landed Mandela in jail. He referred to a "small cache of weapons" that had been discovered, along with "papers" that incriminated Mandela in some plot. He said Mandela and several others were subsequently "charged with sabotage and seeking to overthrow the government by force." Robinson added, "Mandela did not deny the charges. Instead, he used the trial as a forum to explain to the world why government repression had left no choice but armed struggle to achieve democracy."

According to Robinson, at the trial Mandela said, "I have cherished the ideal of a democratic and free society in which all persons live together in harmony and with equal opportunities. It is an ideal I hope to live for and achieve. But if need be, it is an ideal for which I am prepared to die for."

Robinson's references to a "small cache of arms" and Mandela's pro-democracy statements provided an extremely misleading impression of what Mandela was found guilty of and what he stands for. Court records show that Mandela and the other saboteurs had planned the manufacture of at least seven types of bombs, 48,000 anti-personnel mines and 210,000 hand grenades. Mandela himself admitted that they had planned the "destruction of power plants, and interference with rail and telephone communications," in an effort to "scare away capital from the country" and destabilize the economy.

At the trial, Mandela may have made noises about being for democracy. But he also stated that he had been "influenced by Marxist thought," and that "some form of socialism" was needed in South Africa. John Lofton and Cal Thomas, the last American journalists to have interviewed Mandela, reported that while he denies he is a communist, he nevertheless believes that communism is "better" than the current system in South Africa, that communism "gives equal opportunity to everybody," and that under communism "everybody would be living better."

These pro-communist statements were ignored in the PBS program about Mandela. There was also no mention of the fact that the ANC today is dominated by communists. The organization's executive secretary, Alfred Nzo, is a member of the South African Communist Party, as are most members of the ANC's executive committee.

When the PBS program wasn't whitewashing Nelson Mandela, it was portraying his wife, Winnie, in a favorable light. What went completely ignored is the fact that Winnie Mandela has endorsed the use of "necklacing" against her political opponents. This is when radical blacks place a tire laced with gasoline around the neck of a moderate black. The tire and victim are then set ablaze. It is South Africa's version of a lynching.

"With our necklaces," Winnie Mandela had declared, "we shall liberate this country." This statement makes ANC president Oliver Tambo seem like a moderate in comparison. He has said about necklacing, "I regret it, but I cannot condemn it."

January 9, 1987

195

"60 Minutes" Lies About Chile

Mike Wallace's blatant falsehoods mislead public

It is obvious that Chile is on the media's target list, along with South Africa. And in each case, it is being alleged that the U. S. must assist in the destabilization of the government because it violates human rights. The fact that each government is under assault by the forces of international communism is beside the point. It is also irrelevant that destabilization could lead to the coming to power of a Communist government that violates human rights to an even greater degree.

On November 23rd, the CBS program *60 Minutes* used the human rights stick against the government of Chile. It was an emotional and shocking story about two young adults in Chile who were severely burned during a confrontation with the Chilean army. One of them, a resident of the United States, later died. Correspondent Mike Wallace called the burnings only one of the latest of a tragically long list of human rights violations charged to the regime of General Augusto Pinochet.

He ended the report by suggesting the U. S. had acted hypocritically when it abstained from voting on a World Bank loan to Chile, but had previously voted against such a loan to Nicaragua. Wallace didn't point out the obvious—that Chile is an anti-communist nation friendly to the United States, while Nicaragua is hostile. As such, there is no legitimate reason to create economic problems for Chile.

Wallace introduced the story about the burnings by noting that General Pinochet has ruled Chile since 1973, when he took power after a military coup. Wallace described it as a coup "aided by the CIA." But that is a blatant falsehood. A

196

Senate committee headed by liberal Senator Frank Church investigated the circumstances surrounding that coup and found no evidence that the CIA was directly involved in it.

The other big lie perpetuated by Wallace was that the two young people burned during the confrontation with the Chilean army were innocent victims. Wallace admitted that they were on their way to an anti-government protest, involving the building of street barricades that are doused with gasoline and set on fire with small bottles filled with inflammable liquid. But he does not acknowledge the evidence that one of them, Rodrigo Rojas, was carrying one of those bottles, better known as a molotov cocktail. This evidence, consisting of statements made by lawyers for Rojas's mother and a witness to the incident, was reported by *The Washington Post* several weeks before the *60 Minutes* story aired. Wallace acted as if he was unaware of it.

Instead, what Wallace reported was that General Pinochet had suggested that the burning had been an accident, that Rojas had burned himself and the woman with him with a molotov cocktail that he had been carrying. Wallace dismissed this, saying that lawyers involved in the case had said that "any such bomb would have been seized well before the burning occurred."

But that is not clear at this point. NBC's *1986* program last August did a report on the burnings that quoted Chilean officials as saying that the woman with him had kicked one of the bottles of flammable liquid and had set them both on fire. The truth, of course, is not yet in. The Chilean government is currently investigating the incident. What is clear is that *60 Minutes* decided to present only one side of the story.

December 9, 1986

197

The Media
Try To Destroy
The President

UPI reporter Helen Thomas' brutal confrontation with the President

Washington Times editorial cartoonist Bill Garner captured the spirit of the President's recent news conference on Iran with a cartoon showing the President having slipped into an alley while a reporter with a hangman's noose runs down the street after him. "That was close," Reagan says. But in the shadows stood a big brute.

Some Republicans have come to the defense of the President. Senator Larry Pressler of South Dakota said that the press corps was "dripping with venom" in its desire to politically destroy the President. Senator Jesse Helms of North Carolina said he was ashamed of the way the media savaged the President during his news conference. Helms said "the President deserves more respect than that."

Senator Helms' reaction was shared by many people. Accuracy in Media received a number of complaints about the media's performance during that news conference. Some of the complaints came from journalists themselves. The reporters at the news conference had every right to ask tough and probing questions. But the questions sometimes appeared to be nothing more than political charges designed to embarrass and discredit the President.

UPI reporter Helen Thomas, for example, asked the following question: "How would you assess the credibility of your own administration in the light of the prolonged deception of Congress and the public in terms of your secret dealings with Iran, the disinformation, (and) the trading of Sakharov for Daniloff?" Before letting the President answer, Thomas informed him that she would have a follow-up.

Thomas' question was itself very unprofessional, even rude and abrasive. She did not ask him to respond to charges of deception raised by anybody in particular, she herself made the charge of deception. This is certainly not appropriate for a reporter who is supposed to be a professional journalist, free from political bias. The same complaint can be leveled against ABC White House reporter Sam Donaldson, who used his question of the President to accuse him of "duplicity."

When the President was asked for the third time about his credibility, whether he could repair the damage that had been done, the President reacted somewhat angrily, saying, "I imagine I'm the only one around who wants to repair it and I didn't have anything to do with damaging it."

Regardless of what one may think about the Iran policy, it must be granted that the President had a point. The media overkill during his news conference was extraordinary. Images of reporters as a lynch mob or snakes eager to strike and kill their victim did not seem to be overly dramatic.

This media frenzy accelerated when the President revealed on November 25th that national security adviser John Poindexter and Lieutenant Colonel Oliver North of his staff had been relieved of their duties in connection with the Iran policy. It was alleged that North had diverted funds paid by Iran for the arms from the U. S. to the cause of freedom fighters in Nicaragua. Reporters quickly suggested that North had broken the law and that a scandal was enveloping the White House. Not even the Democratic leaders of the House and Senate were prepared to go that far.

December 5, 1986

Cagney And Lacey Go To South Africa

Network program again is used for propaganda

The November 24 episode of the popular CBS program *Cagney and Lacey*, was advertised as the first attempt by a dramatic series to deal with today's "hottest conflict" - South Africa. But it generated more heat than light. Viewers were told that it was a simple case of whites oppressing blacks, and there were no communists involved. The solution was to "boycott" or disinvest from South Africa.

Detectives Cagney and Lacey were given the assignment of protecting a white South African runner who was kidnapped in an effort to force her out. As viewers presumably watched and waited to see how it would all turn out, the producers of the program slipped an assortment of propaganda messages into the script.

The most ludicrous claim made by several characters was that South Africa treats blacks like Nazi Germany treated the Jews. Almost as outrageous was the statement by Detective Lacey that South African blacks don't have "any rights at all." Black rights are certainly limited, but no one can seriously say they don't have any rights. Moreover, those rights are expanding under the reformist government of South African President P. W. Botha.

There were no references in the program to "necklacing," the lynching by fire of moderate blacks by radical blacks. But the South African government, which has tried to prevent such lynchings, was graphically accused of gross human rights violations. In one scene, Cagney and Lacey went to the headquarters of an anti-South Africa group and met a black woman and her son. She told the detectives that her husband was killed by the security forces in South Africa

200

and that she was "thrown in solitary confinement" for eleven months just because she went to his funeral.

To make matters worse, she said "the police broke my son's head open," for no apparent reason. "They sewed him up with nothing for the pain," she said. "They made me listen to him scream." *Cagney and Lacey* reacted with shock and horror when the boy took off his stocking cap to reveal a huge scar on his head.

Another propaganda message was that those against disinvestment are only interested in protecting their business interests. Lacey's husband, Harvey, charged that the "multinational companies don't want us to boycott South Africa" because of the minerals there. "Big business won't let us take a stand on this apartheid stuff," Harvey added, "What South Africa's got, they need." Are any of these minerals important for America's national defense? Not according to Harvey. He said they only go into "toasters, faucets, whatever."

Ironically on the very day this program aired, South African Zulu Chief Gatsha Buthelezi was in the United States reaffirming his opposition to disinvestment. He cited evidence—not even alluded to in the program—that the majority of South Africa's blacks oppose disinvestment because it will hurt them economically.

The program also ridiculed those, like President Reagan, who have warned that the Communists are trying to take advantage of the unrest in South Africa. During a discussion between two other detectives, one of them, a white man, said that "the Communists are using the black people to take over the country." The other detective, a black man, reacted with dismay at such a naive view. The blacks, he insisted, are just fighting to be "free people."

One note of sanity in the program was a statement by a South African runner who did withdraw from the marathon. Addressing the detectives as representatives of the U. S., he said, "You people amaze me. You throw all your moral posturing at us. And then you turn around and trade with East Germany, where everyone's a slave. At least in South Africa we're trying." Detective Cagney's articulate response, "Give me a break."

The runner had a point that the producers apparently felt compelled to state but were unable to rebut. The U. S. boycotts South Africa but continues to trade not only with East Germany but with the Soviet Union itself.

In case you were wondering, the kidnapper turned out to be the runner's trainer, who wanted to keep the boy from returning to South Africa, where he would "learn to hate."

November 26, 1986

CNN Correspondent Suffers Major Embarrassment

His flawed reporting blasted by U.S. Ambassador

Cable News Network, CNN, calls itself the world's most important network. It has a reputation for providing both sides of an issue and in depth coverage. But, in an unusual development, CNN was recently forced to give a critic an opportunity to come on the air and comment on the network's coverage. The result was that CNN's coverage was exposed as seriously deficient and misleading.

The CNN correspondent is Stuart Loory, who served as the network's Moscow bureau chief from 1982 until a few months ago. Prior to returning to the United States and becoming a senior correspondent, Loory traveled throughout the Soviet-bloc. His reports on various communist countries are now airing daily on CNN's *International Hour*. But his reports on Communist Rumania were so flawed that David Funderburk, the former U. S. Ambassador to Rumania, called up CNN and Loory vigorously to protest. His complaint resulted in an invitation to appear on CNN and rebut Loory personally.

In one report, Loory had claimed that Rumanian President Nicolai Ceausescu had cultivated the respect of his people and also their fear. But the rest of the report was devoted only to how he had supposedly cultivated their respect by authorizing the construction of huge building projects and by acting independently of Moscow in foreign affairs. Funderburk, the former U. S. Ambassador to Rumania, used his appearance on CNN to plead with Loory to "look beneath the surface." He said the Rumanian and Soviet governments have a policy of making it appear that Rumania is independent of the Soviet bloc, in order to get favored treatment from the West. Funderburk said the reality is that the Soviets and the Rumanians collaborate in economic, intelligence and other matters.

Although Loory had emphasized that Rumania doesn't take part in Warsaw Pact maneuvers, and doesn't allow Soviet troops on its soil, Funderburk said that Soviet troops have in fact crossed through Rumania territory, that Rumania votes with the Soviets at the United Nations, and that a Rumania defector had implicated Rumania in a scheme to smuggle high technology goods out of the West into the Soviet Union.

Funderburk accused Loory of basically whitewashing human rights abuses by the regime by claiming that the Jews in the country were well-treated and allowed to emigrate. Funderburk said they are only well-treated in comparison to other religious groups that are severely persecuted. He said the freedom to emigrate is conditioned on the Israeli government paying the Rumanian government a certain price to allow each person out. The former ambassador said that the World Human Rights Guide, published by the respected British publication *The Economist*, had identified Rumania and the Soviet Union as among the five worst human rights violators in the world today.

Ironically, on the very day that one of Loory's reports on Rumania was airing, CNN's owner Ted Turner was telling a group in Washington that he hadn't heard any criticism of CNN, even from the furthest members of the right wing. We don't know if he tuned in on the day that former Ambassador Funderburk exposed and debunked the myths that his reporter Loory had tried to perpetuate about Rumania.

November 24, 1986

NBC Blames
Reagan For Summit Failure

Tom Brokaw misleads viewers about Reagan-Gorbachev meeting in Reykjavik, Iceland

In trying to explain what happened in Reykjavik, Iceland, NBC *Nightly News* anchorman Tom Brokaw said the Soviets made a demand that was unacceptable to President Reagan. It was that, for ten years, testing of "Star Wars" or the Strategic Defense Initiative would be limited to the laboratory. No space tests would be allowed. Brokaw said, "President Reagan would not accept that limit on 'Star Wars,' even when Gorbachev agreed to remove all ballistic missiles during that ten year period." The use of the phrase, "even when," had the effect of making President Reagan appear unreasonable and uncompromising.

Later, Brokaw introduced a report on what he called Gorbachev's side of the story. It was not that different from NBC's side of the story. Reporter Phil Bremen said that the Soviet news media were busy underscoring Gorbachev's position that a breakthrough toward a safer world was lost because of the American desire to put weapons in space.

NBC White House correspondent Chris Wallace pointed out in his report that president Reagan had offered "a bold plan of his own." The president said the U. S. would not deploy "Star Wars" for ten years in return for elimination of ballistic missiles on both sides. Wallace reported that Gorbachev said that was not enough, and made it clear progress on all other issues depended on resolving "Star Wars."

In light of what Wallace himself reported, NBC could have opened that news broadcast differently. Tom Brokaw could have said, "Soviet leader Gorbachev would not accept the elimination of ballistic missiles on both sides, even though President Reagan agreed to prohibit deployment of 'Star Wars' for ten years." If phrased in this way, it would have had the effect of making Soviet leader Gorbachev appear unreasonable and uncompromising. The NBC *Nightly News* with Tom Brokaw chose not to present the news in that manner. It decided to make President Reagan look bad. Although reporter Chris Wallace knew better, he tried to add to that impression by claiming that aides to the president said that he was personally aware that "many in Europe and this country blame him for the summit failure."

We truly doubt if any aide to the president had made such a statement. That's because it was simply not true. The only ones eager to blame the president were the Soviets. ABC's *World News Tonight* reported that European leaders were standing behind President Reagan and that politicians on Capitol Hill were generally reluctant to criticize him. The CBS *Evening News* said that while the Europeans were disappointed, they were hopeful about the future of U. S.-Soviet relations. CBS News reporter Bob Faw said, ". . . even his political opponents went to great lengths not to criticize him." He surveyed the Senate races in California, North Carolina, Washington and Florida, and didn't find one Democratic candidate willing to attack the president.

Tom Brokaw said that the president, in his speech to the nation, tried to "defend his actions." It was as if NBC had found President Reagan guilty of committing a crime. It was the kind of coverage one expected from the Soviet media.

October 22, 1986

206

PBS Insults
Cuban Lovers
Of Freedom

How, in some programs, PBS hides shocking truth about brutal Cuban prisons

At the end of September, PBS aired a documentary titled, *Cuba—In the Shadow of Doubt*, which can best be described as propaganda for the Castro regime. We pointed out in our last broadcast that it was aired shortly after publication of an important book by the Cuban poet, Armando Valladares, about the twenty-two years he spent in Fidel Castro's prisons for the crime of expressing anti-communist sentiments. The book is titled, "Against All Hope," and it has earned Valladares the title of "Cuba's Solzhenitsyn."

What the book says about Cuban prisons is in sharp contrast to the impression given by the PBS documentary, which was funded with $185,000 of the taxpayers' money. The film takes us on a guided tour of the Havana Women's Prison. The narrator says: "We hoped to film political prisoners, but we were told that there were none at the facility."

Of course. Fidel Castro has declared that there are no political prisoners in Cuba. Valladares was told by a member of Castro's Political Police: "You are not political prisoners. You are counter revolutionaries. In socialist countries there are no political prisoners." Castro tried to eliminate any reminder that there were political prisoners in his jails by trying to force them to wear the same blue uniforms worn by ordinary criminals. When the political prisoners refused to wear the blue uniforms, they were brutally beaten. When they still refused, they were given the choice of the blue uniforms or nothing.

Valladares and several hundred of his brave comrades went naked, even in the cold weather, rather than permit Castro to erase the distinction between them and oridinary criminals. A good part of his book is taken up with descriptions of the incredible tortures inflicted on these resisters, many of whom were released from prison and permitted to come to the United States only days before PBS aired its film showing a clean, neat prison, where all the inmates were dressed in blue, and where they accepted the story that there were no political prisoners.

October 16, 1986

Another Marxist Message From PBS

PBS program, "Cuba, In The Shadow of Doubt," gives falsified and distorted view . . . again

Our *Public Broadcasting Service* seems to have decided to dedicate 1986 as the year of Marxist propaganda. By my count, which may be incomplete, PBS had already given us six leftist documentaries and one leftist musical in 1986 before it began airing the nine-part series *The Africans*. That might be sub-titled, *Africa Through the Eyes of a Marxist-Anti-imperialist*.

Squeezed in between *Seeing Red: The Stories of American Communists*, which aired on September 10 and *The Africans*, which began its run on October 7, we were given one hour of pro-Castro propaganda titled *Cuba: In the Shadow of Doubt*. This documentary, which the taxpayers funded with $175,000 from the Corporation for Public Broadcasting and $10,000 from the New York Council for the Humanities, is virtually a showcase for Fidel Castro. It does include interviews with a few of Castro's critics—none of them as well-known as Armando Valladares, whose recently published book, *Against All Hope*, tells of the 22 years he spent in Castro's prisons. Valladares has become known as Cuba's Solzhenitsyn.

His book has stirred even such inveterate defenders of left-wing dictators as columnist Mary McGrory to utter a few unkind words about Castro. PBS exhibited the most extraordinary chutzpah in airing, in the wake of the publication of this devastating volume, a film that actually gives us a guided tour through one of Castro's prisons and makes it appear to be a model correction institution that would pass any inspection by Amnesty International or the International Red Cross. The guide has the gall to say, "We have nothing to hide. Where else in the world can you film the prison like you're doing here?'' There is no rejoinder provided by the producers of this mendacious documentary, nor do they point out that Castro does not permit the Red Cross or any reputable human rights group to inspect his prisons, even though they permit the guide to give that impression. She says the prison is visited by foreigners—East German instructors in torture, perhaps?

The viewers of this documentary will learn some badly distorted history of Cuba and U.S.-Cuban relations. For example, it says that nearly 20,000 Cubans were killed in Cuba's cities in the struggle to overthrow Batista. The producers were perhaps unaware of a famous letter written by Miguel Angel Quevedo, the former editor of the Cuban magazine *Bohemia*, which cast new light on these 20,000 deaths. Quevedo, who had helped bring Castro to power, went into exile after he discovered that Fidel was taking Cuba down the communist path. Before committing suicide in Venezuela, he wrote a bitter letter about who was responsible for the tragedy of Cuba.

He assigned a lot of the blame to journalists, including himself and his magazine. He said that the journalists had covered up Castro's participation in the communist "Bogatazo" riots that left 1,500 persons dead in Bogota, Colombia in 1948 and his "gangster-like conduct" when he was a student at the University of Havana. (The PBS documentary also omitted these aspects of Castro's career.) He went on to say, "*Bohemia* was nothing more than the echo of the street, a street contaminated with hate, that applauded *Bohemia* when *Bohemia* invented 'the 20,000 deaths.' "

There is very little in this propaganda piece that is not falsified or distorted, but special attention is given to covering up the facts about the mess the communists have made of the Cuban economy. The film starts off talking about how bad it was that in the old days Cuba was so dependent on sugar. The impression was given that Castro was going to change that. It was never pointed out that Cuba is just as dependent on sugar as its principal export as it ever was. Taiwan was just as dependent on sugar exports as Cuba in 1960, but it has since become a very successful producer and exporter of manufactured goods. In the process it has enormously lifted the living standards of its people. The documentary suggests that Cuba has succeeded economically, but the truth is that it has been a miserable failure, sustained only by massive Soviet aid.

October 3, 1986

The Media Don't Tell All About Bishop Tutu

How his real record is kept from the U.S. public by the news media

Bishop Desmond Tutu is undoubtedly the best known black South African as far as the American people are concerned. Our media have made him more famous here than he is in South Africa. He has been described by one columnist as the most influential black in South Africa. Another report said that he headed the second largest Christian Church there. A Nobel Peace Prize winner, he has been portrayed as a moderate and as a foe of violence.

Other South African clergymen, both white and black, are both amused and disturbed by what they say is the false impression that Americans have about Bishop Tutu's influence in South Africa. They point out that the Anglican Church, which Tutu will head as the Archbishop of Capetown, accounts for less than five percent of all South Africans. It ranks as the fifth largest denomination in the country, and its members include only 132,000 blacks, according to the 1980 census. This compares to over one million blacks who belong to the Dutch Reformed Church and over 4 million who belong to the Independent Black Churches.

Bishop Tutu's following among South African blacks has been greatly exaggerated by our media. His strong support for sanctions against South Africa has been interpreted here as representing the views of South Africa's blacks. According to the BBC, however, two recent polls indicate that sanctions are opposed by about three-quarters of the blacks. Another poll conducted by the *London Sunday Times* found that only

212

29 percent of the blacks support sanctions while the rest are either opposed or have no opinion on the issue.

It is also unfortunate that the media have neglected to say much, if anything, about some of Bishop Tutu's more revealing remarks. On August 15, United Press International reported that Tutu has said during his visit to Peking that Communist China would "provide a very good model for developing countries." He told reporters that he longs for South Africa to adopt "the caring, the compassion, which seem to be coming" in Communist China. He added that among the features of Chinese communism that impressed him was the fact that they allowed for differing points of view.

The Bishop confessed to reporters that he was not aware that several priests in China are imprisoned as dangerous "counter-revolutionaries." We wonder if this man of peace has any idea of the number of millions who have been slaughtered by the Chinese communists. Mao Tse-Tung is listed in the Guinness Book of World Records as history's greatest mass murderer. The slaughter goes on today, as China imposes capital punishment for relatively minor crimes and has executed thousands routinely.

But Bishop Tutu himself is not so dedicated to non-violence as his Nobel Peace Prize might lead one to believe. Two years ago, he made this incredible statement: "Imagine what would happen if only 30 percent of domestic servants (in white South African households) would poison their employers' food." Some interpreted that as a threat. Others as a possible suggestion. When radical blacks began murdering moderate blacks in 1984, Bishop Tutu threatened to leave the country if the lynchings didn't stop. Since then, they have increased and have become far more brutal. Bishop Tutu has forgotten about his threat to leave the country to protest this barbarism.

September 9, 1986

Television Misreports Tennessee Textbook Case

Liberal reporters intentionally mislead public

On September 24th closing arguments will be heard in the Tennessee textbook case known as *Scopes II*. If your understanding of this case is based on how it's been reported in the media, you probably think it's a contest between the local school board and a group of fundamentalist Christian parents who want to ban certain books from their children's school and who want to impose their beliefs on others. This is a gross distortion of the case.

Television news has performed miserably in reporting on the case, with ABC the most notorious. A July 14th report by Al Dale on ABC's *World News Tonight* claimed that the parents were suing the school board because they didn't want their children to read stories such as *Goldilocks and the Three Little Pigs*. He also claimed they objected to a textbook illustration that showed a little girl reading a book and a little boy cooking because it reversed traditional sex roles. In fact, the parents have not objected to any of this in their suit. What's more, reporter Al Dale was told they had no objection before his report was aired.

Rebecca Hagelin of Concerned Women for America has been trying her best to correct the errors and distortions about the case that have appeared in the media. CWA is providing legal counsel for the parents in their suit. She says the parents, in their suit, are objecting to stories that they believe violate their religious beliefs. For example, they say one story portrays suicide in a positive manner, and another promotes one world government. They say the teacher's edition of one of the readers provides instructions for children to write witchcraft incantations and participate in eastern-style meditation exercises.

The information about the parents' alleged objection to a girl reading and a boy cooking was also picked up by CBS reporter Bob Faw and NBC reporter Bob Abernathy in stories they did on the case. But CBS *Evening News* anchorman Dan Rather was guilty of a more serious error. He introduced Faw's story by claiming that the parents wanted to "ban" certain textbooks from the schools. But reporter Faw contradicted Rather by pointing out that this was "no ordinary censorship case." He said, "No one wants to ban or burn anything." He noted that the parents only want a different set of books for their children—books already approved by the state of Tennessee.

Reporter Bob Faw should also be congratulated for making another important point. He noted that the reading books in question, those objected to by the parents, are published by Holt, Rinehart and Winston, a subsidiary of CBS.

Concerned Women for America was so angry with some coverage of the case that it issued a press release accusing the national media of providing the public with inaccurate information. CWA founder and President Beverly LaHaye says, "The American public would be enraged if they only knew how the opposition and the press have clouded the real issues here. (The plaintiffs) merely want the court to recognize their children's right to opt out of reading classes that violate their religious beliefs, and their right to have an alternate reader which does not violate their beliefs."

September 3, 1986

215

How TV
Journalists
Editorialize

One-sided reporting completely distorts the truth about South Africa

When television journalists are accused of inserting their own opinions into their news reports, they usually respond angrily that they only report the news. They deny that they editorialize. Strictly speaking, that's true. NBC's Chris Wallace or ABC's Sam Donaldson don't come on camera and tell the viewers *their* opinion of the president's speech on South Africa. All they do is interview other people who tell what they thought of the speech. But in selecting the people whose opinions will be aired on the evening news, the networks can themselves make a strong editorial statement.

When President Reagan delivered his speech on the administration's policy toward South Africa on July 22, he displeased the liberals who want to see the United States adopt tough, punitive sanctions against South Africa. He didn't entirely please conservatives who thought that he went too far in pandering to the liberal clamor for pressure on the South African government. For example, he said that Nelson Mandela, who is in prison for terrorist activities, should be released even though Mandela has spurned President Botha's offer to release him if he will renounce violence.

The networks made it clear which side they were on. In reporting reactions to the president's speech, CBS interviewed Senator Edward M. Kennedy and Congressman William Gray, two liberal Democrats who are pressing hard for the sanctions the President opposes. To get a South African's reaction, CBS arranged for a telephone interview with the Rev. Alan Boesak, one of the leaders of the militant blacks who favor sanctions. The network also reported that Senator

216

Richard Lugar, the Republican who chairs the Senate Foreign Relations Committee was disappointed with the speech. The one voice that CBS presented on the other side was the South African ambassador to the United States, Herbert Beukes.

NBC also went to Senator Kennedy and a liberal Democratic Congresswoman, Barbara Boxer, for reactions. From South Africa, they succeeded in getting the American media's favorite South African black, Bishop Desmond Tutu, who was so unhappy with President Reagan that he said as far as he was concerned the West "could go to hell." They also reported that three Republican senators were unhappy with the speech—Lugar, Nancy Kassebaum of Kansas and William Roth of Delaware. They couldn't find anyone on the other side, not even the South African ambassador.

It isn't that the networks could not have found Americans who would have supported the president's position or who might have criticized him for going too far to appease the clamor from the left for sanctions. The White House says that on the day of the speech, phone calls supporting the president outnumbered those that were critical by five to one. Supporters in Congress could easily have been found.

Many people were angered and shocked by Bishop Tutu's intemperate "go-to-hell" outburst, but none of our networks aired any critical comments about that. A year ago, when the Rev. Jerry Falwell called Tutu a phony for purporting to represent the majority of South African blacks, NBC showed what it thought by interviewing three people who condemned Falwell. It reveals its position now by airing no criticism of Tutu.

August 7, 1986

The Row
Over
Rehnquist

*The media attack his Supreme Court nomination by
emphasizing false charges*

When President Reagan announced on June 17 that he
was nominating Justice William Rehnquist to succeed Warren
E. Burger as Chief Justice of the United States, conservatives
cheered. The liberal reaction was subdued. They disliked
Rehnquist's conservatism, which had been reflected consistently in his votes and opinions during the 15 years he had
served as associate justice, but they had to acknowledge his
talent as a jurist and his probity. It was recognized that this
was an appointment that would be hard to stop.

That didn't keep the diehards at *The Washington Post*
from trying. One month after the announcement of the nomination, The Post launched a massive attack on Justice Rehnquist. The first article, which began on page one and filled a
full page inside the paper, was an effort to show that 34 years
ago, when Rehnquist was a young law clerk for Justice
Robert Jackson, he held views on controversial issues, such
as the "separate-but-equal" doctrine, that are beyond the pale
today. It tried to show that Rehnquist had not been truthful in
his 1971 confirmation hearing when he said that a memo
defending "separate but equal" had been prepared at Jackson's request and had reflected the Justice's views, not his
own.

The Post's efforts were undercut when Donald Cronson,
who was a clerk for Jackson at the same time as Rehnquist,
confirmed that Jackson had requested a memo defending the
segregationist doctrine and that both he and Rehnquist had
worked on it. Cronson said that he personally thought "separate but equal" was wrong. He said that Rehnquist, as a law

218

clerk, had defended all kinds of outrageous things "which I know he didn't believe." He said the whole thing was a silly issue that was irrelevant to Rehnquist's qualifications to become chief justice. The Post reported this, but the headline and the lead said that Rehnquist had defended "separate but equal." Cronson's statement that the young law clerk liked to defend outrageous positions that he didn't really believe was relegated to the next-to-last paragraph.

The Post and a small group of liberal Democrats revived a charge that Rehnquist had harassed minority voters in Phoenix in 1962. The charge had been rejected by the Judiciary Committee when it considered Rehnquist's appointment to the Court in 1971. New witnesses had been found to challenge the justice's denial that he had personally engaged in challenging voters.

It turned out that the credibility of these witnesses left a lot to be desired. Two of them, Dr. Sidney Smith and James J. Brosnahan, were tripped up when they appeared before the Judiciary Committee to testify against Rehnquist when it was brought out that their sworn testimony differed from what they had previously told reporters.

The Washington Post had reported that Brosnahan, an assistant U. S. attorney in Phoenix in 1962, had gone to investigate complaints about Republican challenges at Bethune precinct. It said: "Brosnahan said he found a small group of Republicans, including Rehnquist, there challenging voters on a random basis, asking Hispanic voters if they could read English and black voters if they could read at all. 'They would do this right in line, rather than getting a person off to the side,' Brosnahan said. 'Telling one person after another, "You can't read," is an aggressive thing to do . . . .'"

But before the committee, Brosnahan couldn't remember what precinct this occurred at, nor could he remember the precise nature of the challenges. When Senator Hatch tried to get him to affirm or deny the accuracy of the Post story, Brosnahan ducked.

Smith told the committee that he remembered the exact words he heard Rehnquist tell two black voters because they were "emblazoned" on his mind. However, the account he gave a reporter for National Public Radio was significantly different from his sworn testimony. Dr. Smith told the committee that what he told NPR was "muddled" and that his memory of what he had seen and heard 24 years earlier had improved after he had discussed the matter with his wife, who hadn't even been present.

Most of the media, including *The Washington Post*, failed to report this.

August 1, 1986

Who Is Censoring News From South Africa?

The news media don't report one side of the South Africa story

American journalists have complained loudly about the restrictions on what they can report from South Africa under the state of emergency State President P. W. Botha declared on June 12. They say this prevents them from informing the American people about what is going on in that country. But even while they are complaining about the restrictions on the flow of information imposed by the South African government, our journalists themselves are refusing to tell the American people some important and even sensational news from that country.

In announcing the national state of emergency, President Botha emphasized that the action was being taken because the government had learned of plans being made by radical elements which, he said, posed a real danger for all population groups in the country. He disclosed that in the period from March 1 to June 5, a total of 284 blacks had been killed by black radicals. He said that 172 of these had been killed by the "barbaric, so-called necklace method."

This is lynching by fire. The victim's hands are either hacked off or bound, sometimes with barbed wire. An automobile tire filled with gasoline is hung around the victim's neck and another around the legs. The gasoline is ignited. The hot black smoke from the tire destroys the lining of the victim's throat and lungs. The melting rubber penetrates the flesh. It may take up to twenty minutes for the victim to die an agonizing death. The lynch mob laughs and jeers while this is going on.

What are the terrible crimes that are being punished by

221

this barbarism? According to *Newsweek*, one of the few publications in this country that has described the practice, one of the victims was an old woman who sold funeral insurance. That was considered to be cooperating with the authorities, and she was sentenced to death. Another had given a Christmas party, when the "comrades" had forbidden such celebrations.

If, in a three-month period, there had been 172 lynchings of blacks in the United States by any method, this would have been the biggest news story of the century. Long before the total reached such heights, the TV coverage and the newspaper and magazine stories would have generated such intense public outrage that the Federal government would have been moved to take whatever steps were necessary to halt the killings. If that required a state of national emergency, we would have a state of national emergency. If the lynchings were carried out by the "necklace" method—by burning the victim alive—a single case would have been enough to inflame the country.

How many American viewers of TV news or assiduous readers of our newspapers are aware of the fact that during a three month period an average of two such lynchings occurred each day in South Africa? These haven't been filmed and shown on our television. When President Botha said that there had been 172 such lynchings since last March, our news media didn't even report the figure, much less mention that this was one of the reasons given for declaring the national state of emergency.

Typical of the importance that our human-rights-oriented media have attached to these lynchings, is a report in *The Washington Post* on June 26. This paper ran a 15-paragraph story headlined, "South Africa Warns Journalists To 'Toe the Line' on Coverage." It was devoted to the restrictions imposed on the media by the South African government, except for the last paragraph, which said, "A black man was stabbed to death by a mob in Soweto while another man's burned body was found in a rural part of the Transvaal."

The same spirit of self-censorship has kept our media from reporting that Mrs. Nelson Mandela has encouraged lynching by fire. On April 13, according to an AFP dispatch, she said, "Together, hand in hand with our boxes of matches and necklaces we shall liberate this country." That wasn't mentioned in the adulatory program on Mrs. Mandela aired by PBS, nor was it cited when she was recently given an honorary degree by the John Jay College of Criminal Justice in New York City.

June 27, 1986

Big Lie Admitted But Not Reported

TV and newspaper reporters mislead again about Nicaragua

If any president of the United States, but especially President Reagan, were to admit publicly that he and his top aides had all lied through their teeth for four days about a controversial military operation, that admission would be the lead story on every television newscast and in every daily paper. But when the president of Nicaragua did just that on March 28, CBS News didn't even report it, and our most influential newspapers couldn't quite bring themselves to say that was what President Daniel Ortega had done.

Roger Mudd, who was anchoring the NBC *Nightly News* on March 28, was very clear on the subject. He said: "The government of Nicaragua now admits its troops did cross into Honduras . . . . After steadfastly denying that its troops had crossed the Honduran border, the Sandinista government of Nicaragua admitted today that it had launched military operations in Honduras."

NBC's correspondent in Managua added this information: "Today the government of Nicaragua admitted in convoluted fashion that its soldiers entered Honduras . . . The foreign minister and President Daniel Ortega argue that since Honduras has lost control of its southern border to the Contras, that region is no longer part of Honduras. Ortega says that when his soldiers cross the line that the rest of the world recognizes as Honduras, he's chasing an enemy in a war zone. What's more, says Ortega, since he's not showing aggression toward Honduras, he's not in violation of international law . . . The Nicaraguans say they have wiped out a major Contra training

224

camp in heavy fighting. They say they killed 350 Contras in the last two weeks and lost 40 of their own soldiers.''

The New York Times, in reporting the same story, headlined it: "Nicaragua Leader Warns of Risks in Use of U.S. Forces in Honduras." It said that Ortega had "refused to say whether Nicaraguan troops had crossed into Honduras in recent days, as had been charged by the Reagan administration." The story, by Stephen Kinzer, the Times correspondent in Managua, failed to mention that Ortega had acknowledged that his troops had attacked the training camps of the freedom fighters which are known to be 12 or more miles inside the Honduran border.

The Washington Post did a little better than *The New York Times*, headlining its story: "Ortega Says Contra Areas Have Become 'War Zone'." It said that he had not admitted directly that his troops had entered Honduras, but down in the sixth paragraph of the story, it noted that he had claimed to have occupied and destroyed the main training camp of the freedom fighters and other bases. It reported that Ortega had said these camps were in a "war zone," but he had not disputed that they were on the Honduran side of the border. The attentive reader would have deduced from this that the Sandinistas had been lying about this all week, but the Post did not draw that conclusion for them.

The Philadelphia Inquirer, basing its story on wire service reports, put the Ortega admission that his forces had attacked bases inside Honduras right up in the second paragraph. It pointed out that the Nicaraguans had "managed to avoid openly acknowledging that Sandinista troops had entered Honduras by their redefinition of what they consider to be Honduran territory." This was close to saying that they admitted having lied.

The worst performance of all was by CBS News. It had shown the greatest skepticism about the invasion reports. It had interviewed the Nicaraguan ambassador to the U. N., Nora Astorga, the day before Ortega confessed. She had sworn that no Nicaraguan troops had crossed the border. When her boss revealed that was a big lie, CBS News clammed up. On March 28, instead of reporting Ortega's embarrassing admission, Dan Rather reported that "a senior administration official" had "shrugged off questions about the possibility that President Reagan and his aides may have exaggerated the scope, size and location of the reported Nicaraguan invasion of Honduras this week." Even after Ortega had appeared on CBS's "Face the Nation" and had again admitted attacking the bases, the CBS newscast that night failed to report this information.

April 11, 1986

The
Teflon
Media

How news reporters try to "get" Reagan . . . and how one effort backfired

Former Democratic vice-presidential nominee Geraldine Ferraro and President Reagan have one thing in common: they don't like obnoxious reporters. Reporters crowded around Ferraro recently when she walked to a hearing for her son on charges of selling cocaine. Ferraro called the reporters "vultures," adding: "You people haven't changed." President Reagan was recently besieged by reporters in a White House conference room, where he was posing for pictures with members of a presidential commission. They kept firing questions at him, even though it wasn't supposed to be a news conference. When the reporters were finally ushered out, the president was heard muttering a cuss word. A spokesman later explained that he had only said, "It's sunny and you're rich."

The president was trying to put a funny face on an embarrassing situation. But it wasn't just embarrassing for him; the reporters should have felt ashamed of themselves. Yet the sad fact is that reporters today never seem to apologize for their obnoxious behavior. Reporters can not only be overbearing and intrusive, they can be relentless in their efforts to make someone look like an idiot. No one knows this better than President Reagan, who was asked about it in his recent interviews with Barbara Walters of ABC. The president said the media frequently air criticisms that he doesn't think for himself, that his staff tells him what to do, and that he's always making misstatements. He responded to charges that he's the "teflon president" because the criticisms don't stick to him.

He said the media aren't going to give up on their efforts to make them stick.

The president cited an example. He said he was accused by the media of making six factual errors at a news conference. But he said he had the documentation to back up his statements, and that only one of them could be considered technically wrong. The media used the same ploy after the President gave his national television speech for aid to the Nicaraguan freedom fighters. *The Washington Post*, for example, published a story labeled "news analysis" that purported to identify several "disputed statistics and accusations" in the speech. Reagan was charged with making at least six misstatements.

But two days later, the State Department managed to get a rebuttal to this news analysis published in the Post. The State Department official said that the Post's analysis of the President's speech was "at best disappointing, at worst shocking." In effect, the Post was accused of making more misstatements than the President. And the President's alleged misstatements were shown to be accurate and backed up by the evidence.

The obvious question that needs to be asked is, how could the Post have gotten so mixed up? The answer seems to lie in the Post's hostility toward the President and a strong desire to make him look stupid. In this case, it backfired.

But the Post and other media will continue in their campaign to discredit the President, even if they end up with egg on their faces. It's apparent that the real problem today is not a teflon president, but a teflon media.

April 4, 1986

How Liberal
Journalists
Sling Mud

*Newsweek tries to plant anti-Semitism charge on
Dartmouth College paper*

One of the liberal media's favorite ploys is to brand as
"McCarthyism" any negative information about persons they
like and admire. But the same people who are most apt to cry
"McCarthyism" are often skilled in the art of smearing those
with whom they disagree.

The February 3, 1986 issue of *Newsweek* shows how this
works. A story by *Newsweek's* education editor, Eloise
Salholz, and Shawn Doherty discussed an action by a dozen
Dartmouth students who tore down four shanties that anti-
apartheid protesters had tacked up on the Dartmouth Green.
The article was a pointed attack on conservative Dartmouth
students, particularly those connected with the *Dartmouth
Review*, a conservative campus newspaper.

The *Newsweek* story called the shanties "unsightly," but
labeled the art of tearing them down as "ugly." It referred to
the demolition crew as the "dirty dozen," ten of whom were
linked to the *Dartmouth Review*. *Newsweek* then said that the
campus paper had recently run a piece that "suggested that
admitting more Jews (to Dartmouth) would also devalue the
Dartmouth degree."

This is a very serious charge. But when we called Eloise
Salholz at *Newsweek* to ask her what *Dartmouth Review* story
she was talking about, she refused to discuss it, and suggested
that we take it up with *Newsweek's* lawyers. We explained
that all we wanted to do was get the facts, not file a lawsuit.
Could she provide us with some basis for the statements in the
story? Absolutely not. Ms. Salholz replied that she had no

229

comment on the serious charge against the *Dartmouth Review*.

We told her that we had received a copy of a *Dartmouth Review* article by Adam Lieberman dated November 13, 1985. The article concerned a letter signed by 27 Jewish students, urging the college president to "reject any proposal which would result in a policy of favoritism towards, or segregation of the Jewish student body at Dartmouth." This letter was a reaction to a report that faculty-administration group would soon issue guidelines aimed at raising the 11 percent population of Jewish students at Dartmouth, the lowest in the Ivy League.

The *Dartmouth Review* story was a straightforward account of the reasons for concern over low Jewish enrollment along with the full text of the letter from 27 Jewish students, who felt the proposed guidelines would single out Jews for "favoritism and special treatment." Nothing in this article supported *Newsweek's* claim that the *Dartmouth Review* had suggested that "admitting more Jews would . . . devalue the Dartmouth degree."

The student who sent the *Dartmouth Review* article to Accuracy in Media is a Jewish member of the Review staff. He wrote: "Speaking as a Jew, I can assure you that the Review . . . wouldn't espouse as bigoted a view as *Newsweek* would like to have its readers think." While the student said he didn't agree with all the views of the paper, he felt that *Newsweek* had perpetrated a gross injustice. "The day the Review exhibits such blatant anti-Semitism, or for that matter, bigotry of any kind, would be the day I would leave the paper," he said.

Newsweek ended its story about Dartmouth's shanties by observing that the incident had forced many to "face allegations of bigotry in their own backyard." *Newsweek's* story forces us to face the reality of bigoted, unfair journalism.

February 19, 1986

New Light On
Public's View
Of The Media

Survey by Los Angeles Times twists findings and misleads on public's trust of 'news'

Are the news media suffering from a serious credibility problem? A survey published last year by the American Society of Newspaper Editors cast a pall over that group's annual convention because of its disclosure that a lot of their customers didn't give newspapers high marks. According to this survey fewer than one third of those polled rated newspapers and television high in credibility.

The Los Angeles Times has now published a new survey which comes to exactly the opposite conclusion. It finds that "the vast majority of the citizenry thinks the major news organizations in America are believable." Asked to rate major news organizations, over 80 percent of the respondents classified such news organizations as CBS, NBC, ABC, *Time*, *Newsweek*, *The Wall Street Journal*, *The Associated Press*, local newspapers, local TV news and radio news as either "believable" or "highly believable," it says.

Individual television news personalities did even better in these ratings. Retired CBS anchorman Walter Cronkite was judged believable or highly believable by 92 percent of the respondents, while other network news anchormen or former anchormen were in the 88 percent to 90 percent range.

This was welcomed as good news by the media. *The New York Times* headlined the story, "Poll Finds 'No Credibility Crisis' for News Media." *The Washington Post* led its story with the statement that "Americans give the news media high marks for credibility and competence."

But analysis of the *Los Angeles Times* poll, which was done for the paper by the Gallup organization, tells quite a different story. The key question about believability was seriously flawed, and the answers to it were presented in a way that was highly misleading.

Those polled were asked to rate the believability of the media organizations and prominent journalists on a scale of 4 to 1, with "4" meaning "you can believe all or most of what they say" and "1" meaning "you can believe almost nothing of what they say." Unfortunately, they were not told what "2" and "3" meant, which the poll designers acknowledge was a mistake. In writing up the results, "2" was labeled "believable," which may or may not be what the respondents had in mind. Bar graphs showed this "believable" together with "4," which was labeled "highly believable." The two categories were totaled to obtain those 80 percent-plus ratings for journalists' "believability."

But see what happens when we focus on how many respondents said that they believed all or most of what the journalists said compared to all other responses. This is not an unreasonable measure of credibility, especially for a profession whose stock in trade is supposed to be honesty and accuracy.

We find that only about one-third of those responding believed all or most of what they saw on the three network news shows and in *Time* and *Newsweek*. Only 25 percent believed all or most of what they read in nationally influential newspapers, except for *The Wall Street Journal*. The Journal scored higher than any other news source, with 45 percent saying they believed most or all of what it printed. It was closely followed by the *MacNeil/Lehrer News Hour* on PBS, which garnered a 43 percent vote of confidence.

The prominent journalists suffer a similar decline in their credibility when held to this not unreasonably higher standard. Only 44 percent believe the CBS anchorman, Dan Rather, measures up to that standard, and NBC's Tom Brokaw was that convincing to only 37 percent. ABC's Peter Jennings was in between at 40 percent.

The only strictly print journalist included was the muckraking columnist Jack Anderson, who was given a 17 percent rating for high credibility.

What this means is that 65 percent of those polled do not agree with the statement that one can believe all or most of what they see on TV news programs or read in most newspapers and news magazines. This finding is not too different from that of the ASNE poll last year, the one that caused alarm in journalistic circles.

January 17, 1986